THE TRUTH ABOUT AARON

THE TRUTH ABOUT AARON

MY JOURNEY TO UNDERSTAND MY BROTHER

JONATHAN HERNANDEZ

WITH LARS ANDERSON

HARPER

An Imprint of HarperCollins*Publishers*

Certain names and identifying details have been changed to protect the privacy of the individuals involved.

HarperCollins books may be purchased for educational, business, or sales promotional use. For information, please email the Special Markets Department at SPsales@harpercollins.com.

FIRST EDITION

Library of Congress Cataloging-in-Publication Data has been applied for.

ISBN 978-0-06-287271-5

18 19 20 21 22 LSC 10 9 8 7 6 5 4 3 2 1

For anyone who has experienced pain

PREFACE

To many, my younger brother, Aaron Josef Hernandez, was a monster. I understand how some people could think he got the fate he deserved. He definitely caused destruction in my life, and I'm only now beginning to understand the meaning and impact of his actions.

After Aaron was found guilty of murder, I found myself guilty by association—guilty of being his brother. In May 2015, a month after the jury delivered the verdict, I started going by Jonathan, my middle name, instead of DJ, as I'd always been known. I needed a new beginning. During one of my prison visits, I told Aaron about my name change; he understood why I wanted to do it, given the negative attention focused on him.

Aaron and I talked on the phone at least once a week after his conviction. Over one thousand miles apart, he in a Massachusetts prison and me in Iowa, I could still feel his smile through the phone. In prison he sounded more at peace to me. He was beginning to overcome the inner demons he had been facing—demons that had been growing inside of him long before our father passed away in 2006.

It was painful for both of us when I visited Aaron in person because of the restrictions on our interaction—the shackles on Aaron and the plate of glass between us. Still, while serving his time, Aaron became more reflective and honest with himself about the mistakes he had made and the life he had once led.

"DJ, please embrace life," he said to me during one visit. "Embrace all of what's right in front of you. Please embrace it like it could be gone forever. This is something I wish I would have done."

Moments after he uttered these words, a corrections officer interrupted and said, "Time's up." Aaron had to report back to his cell.

He hung up the phone, stood from his small metal stool, and placed his hand on the glass wall.

"I love you, D," he said.

I matched my palm against his.

"I love you, too, Aaron," I said.

Aaron moved toward the exit door, where the officer awaited him. I walked along with him on the other side of the glass, maintaining eye contact, trying to hold on to our final moments together before he vanished.

AARON WAS A STAR player for the New England Patriots when his NFL career was cut short by his 2013 arrest and 2015 conviction for the murder of Odin Lloyd.

He ended his life two years later. According to prison officials, a corrections officer found Aaron in his cell at Souza-Baranowski Correctional Center in Lancaster, Massachusetts, at 3:03 a.m. on April 19, 2017, lifeless. He had tied a bedsheet around his neck and hanged himself from the window bars. Cardboard had been shoved into the tracks of Aaron's door to prevent it from being opened, and shampoo had been spread across the floor to make it slippery.

They also said that Aaron had a fresh cut on his right middle finger. On his forehead he wrote "John 3:16" in blood. He smeared his blood on the page of the biblical passage that reads: "For God so loved the world, that he gave His one and only Son, that whosoever believes in Him should not perish, but have everlasting life."

At the time of his death, at twenty-seven, Aaron was two years into a life sentence with no chance of parole. Five days earlier, he had been acquitted in a second trial for another murder outside a Boston nightclub a year before Lloyd was killed. I last spoke to my brother just three days before he died. Now I constantly replay the final time I heard his voice.

I was three years older than Aaron. Growing up in Bristol, Connecticut, a city twenty miles southwest of Hartford, we were virtually inseparable. Many evenings we would race each other to the top of a big hill that crested on our street and then, catching our breath, look down at the bright city lights below. Sitting together, we would laugh and talk about our dreams.

There were frightening times, too. During childhood, in the tiny bedroom we shared on Greystone Avenue, I'd wake up in the middle of the night to Aaron's screams.

"They're going to get me!" he'd yell. "They're going to get me!"

Our mother would rush into our bedroom, sit on his bed, and cradle him in her arms as tears streamed down his face. Nothing could soothe him. As she rocked him, he'd keep mumbling, "They're going to get me. They're going to get me."

DURING ONE OF MY final visits with Aaron, he told me, "One day I hope my truth is told." That is the intention of this book, to share the entirety of his story. As painful as this has been for me to relive, no secret will be suppressed, no event will be whitewashed.

Since Aaron's passing, I've reconnected with family members and friends. I've spoken to many of his past associates, law enforcement officials, experts studying the brain disease known as CTE, and former teammates. I've revisited the places of his greatest triumphs and also the scene where Odin Lloyd was murdered. I've reexamined our past together and what led to his double life and his tragic downfall.

Through it all, I've asked myself: Could I have done anything more to help Aaron? Could anyone have saved him?

It is my hope that sharing the truth about Aaron might help others.

THE TRUTH ABOUT AARON

CHAPTER 1

APRIL 19, 2017

THE WINDING COUNTRY ROADS in Connecticut were empty that predawn April morning as I steered my SUV to Ledyard High School, where I was the head football coach.

At 5:05 a.m., I pulled into the empty parking lot and made my way to my classroom on the first floor. One of my volunteers met me in my office to review the goals for our workout with the football team, then, carrying my clipboard with a whistle draped around my neck, I descended two flights of stairs into what some of the older teachers called "the bomb shelter"—the basement of the school that housed our weight and wrestling rooms—to begin the team stretch.

With twenty minutes remaining in the hour-long workout, I looked up and saw Pete Vincent, a physical education teacher, standing in the weight room doorway.

"You have to cancel the workout," he said.

"Why? What's going on?"

"You just have to," he said.

"Pete, let's step outside."

We went into the nearby wrestling room. Pete took a couple of deep breaths, then said, "Aaron passed away this morning. He committed suicide in his prison cell."

My knees buckled and I stumbled to a nearby concrete beam to brace myself. I closed my eyes, trying to process what I had just heard.

"Thank you for telling me, but there is no need to cancel this workout. I can finish."

I clenched my jaw through the remaining ten minutes, then dismissed the team. I was broken. I locked the weight room, turned off the lights, and headed for the door. I needed to get to my mother right away.

I grabbed my bags from my office and racewalked into the mild spring morning to my car. I opened the door, sat behind the wheel, and sobbed like I'd never sobbed before.

When I collected myself, I dialed my mom's number.

"Are you okay?" she asked, an audible catch in her voice.

She told me she had been in her bedroom in her condo getting ready for her day when her husband, watching television on the first floor, screamed for her. She ran down the stairs and saw the news on ESPN.

"I'm coming to see you," I said, as I turned the ignition.

As I drove, the rising sun casting a blush of pink light into the New England sky, I thought about the last time I saw Aaron in prison; I knew something wasn't right. I remembered the paranoia I saw in Aaron during his final days as a free man, the knife he kept on his nightstand, his changing behavior.

I never imagined the depth of the darkness he was falling into.

MY MOTHER MET ME outside on her porch.

"How did it get to this?" I said as we hugged and cried.

We stepped inside and talked for an hour about his suicide because it didn't make sense.

"I can't believe he's gone," I said. "I just can't believe it."

Mentally exhausted, I excused myself to lie down upstairs in the spare bedroom. As soon as I settled under the covers, I heard the front screen door creak open, then slam shut. I bolted out of bed. From the top of the staircase, I could see a reporter peering inside the front-door window. I ran back to the bedroom, looked through the blinds, and saw him returning to the other half-dozen reporters lined up at the end of the street.

When I felt the vibration of the garage door open, I went downstairs to find my mother confronting another reporter. "Get off my property!" she yelled.

Once I felt comfortable leaving my mother alone, I decided to drive back to my apartment in Groton, ninety minutes away. I couldn't wait to hug my wife and our five-month-old daughter. Earlier that morning, I didn't have much time to talk to my wife because of how fast everything was happening.

I left my mother's condo and entered my car. I flipped on the ignition, yanked my sun visor down, and pulled my hooded sweatshirt over my forehead. As I drove away, reporters with notebooks and cameras approached my slow-moving vehicle.

CHAPTER 2

TWENTY YEARS EARLIER

"TIME TO GET UP," our mom said from the foot of my bed where she stood at the ironing board pressing her clothes. She ironed in our room because it was the best space in our small house; she didn't want the board in the middle of the living room for guests to see. "Time to get moving."

I opened my eyes and checked the clock: 6:30 a.m. Aaron was a few feet away on his twin mattress, facedown, mouth open, snoring, with his knees tucked into his chest and his butt up in the air. I was nine and Aaron was six.

Outside the bedroom window, the gray sky was filled with snowflakes, our backyard covered in a sheet of white.

"School's canceled. You're going to the babysitter."

Our mother, Terri, still had to go to work. She was five foot four and 135 pounds, but she had a strong Italian personality and was old-school strict. She was a secretary at our elementary school, less than a mile away.

Our father, Dennis, a five-ten, 240-pound, charismatic Puerto Rican, was a custodian at a middle school in town. He normally worked the late shift, so most mornings as Aaron and I walked through the hallway toward the kitchen we'd see his big belly pushing up the covers on his bed. Today, he was already at the school, plowing the parking lot and shoveling the sidewalks.

Aaron and I brushed our teeth and quickly put on our winter

layers: wool socks, sweatpants, snow pants, and sweatshirts. We headed to the kitchen, where our mother had our lunches packed in two brown paper bags—peanut butter and jelly sandwiches with the crust cut off, fruit, a Twinkie, and an I-love-you note for each of us. We slid on our big puffy coats, our winter hats and boots, and then hopped into our red minivan for the four-minute drive.

These snow days were extra special to us, because when we played football we got to tackle on the unplowed street, no more two-hand touch. That day, we played a pickup game at the end of the cul-de-sac with a couple of the kids from the neighborhood, two-on-two. I was the quarterback and Aaron was my receiver.

In our huddle, I called the plays from our playbook: "Pass in the Grass," "Out to Curb Left," "Double Move to the Basketball Hoop." Aaron ran the route and I flung him the ball. The boys we were playing were older than us but we loved the challenge, especially when they talked trash to us. Our dad always told us not to speak to our opponents, because it was a waste of energy.

The four of us then went tramping through the nearby woods. We climbed trees, played hide-and-seek, and sprinted after each other in our custom winter version of capture the flag: if a snowball hit you in the other team's territory, you had to run back to your flag and touch it before you could rejoin the action.

Around noon it was time to return to our babysitter's house to eat lunch and dry our winter jackets, snow pants, hats, and gloves. We agreed to meet in the street in a few hours for the afternoon rematch.

We ate fast, anxious to return outside. But then one of the older boys at the house, a teenager, asked us to play a game of indoor hide-and-seek. This boy, who was in high school, frightened us. He was a bully and his brother scared us with knives that he flashed at us.

I bolted upstairs, wedging myself into a bedroom closet. Aaron went into a blue tent on the first floor. For five, ten, fifteen minutes, I remained in the dark closet, annoyed. I didn't understand why no one came looking for me.

I found out much later, when Aaron was in prison, that the older boy had actually forced Aaron into the tent.

"Why would the two of you hide in there together?" I asked Aaron that afternoon. "That's not a smart hiding spot."

Aaron didn't say a word.

BACK IN OUR WARM, freshly dried outfits, we were putting our snow boots on near the front door when Aaron said, "Tell me something funny, D. I need to hear something funny, D."

Aaron always asked me to make him laugh when he was upset. I told him a joke and then we went outside to play two-on-two basketball with our friends in the snow at the end of the cul-de-sac. I had no idea what he had just been through.

DINNERTIME WAS AT FIVE o'clock on the dot, so at 4:45 p.m. we started sprinting back home from the babysitter's house, which was a quarter-mile away. If we were late, our dad might take off his leather belt and whip us on the behind with it.

"My legs are killing me," Aaron said. "I can't go faster."

"Hurry, Aaron," I said, struggling for breath. "Hurry."

Our mom greeted us at the front door, looking at her watch. After throwing our winter clothes in the hamper, the four of us—Mom, Dad, Aaron, and myself—sat down at our dinner table in our kitchen, where our mother served us steaming plates of lasagna. After eating, our mother did the dishes and made brownies. Then the four of us piled into our red minivan parked in the driveway. Our destination: Blockbuster Video.

Our dad, riding shotgun, played the green-light game on roads that were now clear of snow. At a red light, he turned to us and said,

"Hey, watch this. I'm a magician. I'll tell you exactly when this red light will turn green."

He counted down from five. Then, seeing the light in the other direction flip from yellow to red, he yelled, "And now!"

We fell for it every time. We were convinced he had super powers.

We weren't the only ones. Our father was beloved in Bristol, where over time he had earned a nickname: The King. Every year he hosted a three-on-three basketball tournament on our backyard court. The grill would be firing, the pig would be roasting, and the cars would be parked up and down the street. Sometimes we'd have five hundred people watching the games, standing shoulder to shoulder, kids on their knees looking between the adults' legs. Others brought lawn chairs and would sit and gossip for hours. Our dad got physical on the court and dominated the grill, where he cooked burgers, hot dogs, and chicken. It was like he was everyone's best friend.

Aaron and I played rock-paper-scissors in the backseat to see who would have first pick of the brownies when we returned home. We both loved the soft center pieces without the crust.

We pulled up to the blue-and-yellow BLOCKBUSTER sign shining in the night. This was our happy place. Aaron and I leaped out of the minivan and ran inside filled with excitement.

We carefully selected our movies to rent before moving to the candy aisle. We each were allowed to make one selection. Everything would be split fifty-fifty.

Once home, we hurried to our room to put on pajamas—white long johns and white tube socks. The four of us had our regular spots on the sectional couch in the living room: Dad was on the far left facing the television, me next to him, then Aaron, then our mother. As the movie started, Aaron and I laid our heads on the same pillow; he stretched his feet over our mother's lap, I put mine over our father's.

For the next few hours, we were just there together, a family, warm in the glow of the television. Our mouths covered in chocolate from the brownies, my brother and I fell asleep on the couch before the second movie began.

THE NEXT MORNING, SATURDAY, began with a basketball game at the local Boys & Girls Club. Aaron was too young for the league, so he sat in the stands eating a sausage-egg-and-cheese sandwich as he cheered my team on. After the final horn, Aaron and I played a game of H-O-R-S-E together until the next team started their pregame layup lines.

As we walked back to our car, I heard my dad say, "Aaron, why do you stand like a faggot—with your hands clasped on your stomach and your elbows glued to your ribs? It's feminine. Are you a faggot? Only faggots stand like that. There are no faggots in the Hernandez family."

Aaron put his head down and he placed his hands straight down by his sides. This wasn't the first and wouldn't be the last time our father grew angry over what he called Aaron's feminine posture.

After dinner, the four of us returned to the living room for our final rented movie when the phone rang. Dad sprang up to answer it.

A few minutes later he reentered the room. "The guys are going out for a few drinks," he told our mother. "I'm going to go with them."

"When will you be home?"

"Ten thirty."

"All right, Dennis," she said with a knowing chuckle.

Around 3 a.m. Aaron and I heard our mom walk past our bedroom to the kitchen, mumbling, "That fucking asshole, that fucking asshole."

We heard her open the side door that led to the driveway. Aaron and I slid out of bed and tiptoed to the kitchen. Aaron took a knee so I could use his thigh as a boost onto the counter to look out the window. Our dad was leaning inside the driver's window talking to his buddies. My mother stood behind him with her arms crossed, yelling.

"Dennis, get your ass inside or get the fuck out of here!"

As our dad turned and started stumbling toward the house, I jumped off the counter, and Aaron and I rushed back to our bedroom. With my head against our cracked bedroom door, I could hear them arguing. I relayed to Aaron what was going on.

"Why the fuck do you have to embarrass me like that in front of my friends!" our father yelled.

Our mom grabbed the rotary phone from the wall and smashed it over his head, shattering the phone into pieces. Then she stubbed the burning ember of her cigarette into his forehead, causing red ashes to fall in the dark.

Our parents shoved their way into the hallway bathroom. Aaron and I snuck out into the hall. We saw our dad slamming our mom's head against the white sink, over and over until she slumped to the ground.

As my dad stood above her, they both looked our way.

"You see this coward, boys?" our mom yelled from the bathroom floor as blood streamed down her forehead. "He's a piece of shit. He thinks he is tough because he can beat a woman."

Aaron and I ran back to our beds. Aaron was crying, so I got on his bed and held him in my arms.

"Say something to make me laugh, D," Aaron whispered.

This time I had nothing to say.

CHAPTER 3

I HATED THE BELT, HATED the hangers, hated my father's hand. Our father would hit us for anything from a bad grade to disrespectful behavior to sheer clumsiness. One morning when I was nine, he lifted me up by my left arm, and, with my legs dangling in the air, spanked me repeatedly, hitting me on the rear end each time he said a word, as was his custom. I always hoped he wouldn't have a lot to say.

Aaron was next to me sobbing as I took my beating for accidently spilling my cereal.

"Are you crying?" my dad asked Aaron.

He dropped me and turned his anger toward Aaron, taking him by the arm and administering another beating. After a few minutes, our dad left the room, leaving Aaron and me on the floor, wiping our tears with our shirts.

Whenever Aaron and I sensed a beating was coming, we ran into our bedroom. As our father got closer, we could hear his footsteps on the wooden floor and his belt buckle clink as he started to take it off. We would crawl underneath our beds and put our backs flush against the wall. Every time he reached for us, we sucked in our stomachs, trying to keep his searching fingertips from grabbing us.

Eventually, he'd become frustrated and leave, saying, "You have to come out of your bedroom at some point."

When it was quiet and we felt safe, Aaron and I would emerge from underneath our beds and embrace each other with tears in our eyes, snot running out of our noses, dust on our shirts and shorts, wondering if we were in the clear. Some days we were; others we weren't.

Once, I told our dad I was going to call the Department of Children and Families, and he handed me the phone before saying, "Call them. As soon as you hang up the phone, I will beat you boys harder than you've ever been beat before. They will have to pull me off of you after they break down the door."

One evening Aaron and I were at the kitchen table trying to finish our homework so we could attend the big high school basketball game with our dad. About a mile from our house, Bristol Central High was hosting crosstown rival Bristol Eastern. I was in eighth grade; Aaron was in fifth.

With tip-off approaching, I worried that I wasn't going to finish in time to make the game. Aaron had completed his assignment and was getting dressed. Nervously, I tapped my pencil on the table as I thought about a question from my homework assignment I was trying to answer.

A few minutes later I mindlessly tapped my pencil again on the table. Just then, I felt something stab into my scalp, two inches above my forehead. I reached up and pulled the two prongs of a vacuum cord out of my head. When the blood began to pour, I started screaming. Aaron ran into the kitchen and started screaming, too. The right side of my face was covered in blood. I thought I was going to die.

I kept a towel pressed against my head for the rest of the night. I didn't make the game.

Late that evening, after Aaron and my dad returned from the game, I heard my parents talking. "It has to stop," my dad said. "It was too close of a call tonight."

CHAPTER 4

SEPTEMBER 12, 2003

It was game day, and we couldn't wait to get on the field.

Aaron and I were just hours away from playing in our first varsity football game together. Aaron was a thirteen-year-old freshman wide receiver and I was a seventeen-year-old senior quarterback at Bristol Central.

That morning I woke up before Aaron. I unraveled the clothes-iron cord from my feet, because my legs hung off the end of my bed and underneath the ironing board my mother used. I sat on the edge of my bed for a few minutes just looking at Aaron sleeping, my best friend. I thought about all the times we had attended high school football games at Muzzy Field in Bristol as children. Under the stadium lights and behind the bleachers, we played tackle football with other kids as the game was going on. When the crowd roared, I'd look at Aaron and tell him, "One day we'll be out there together."

Aaron finally woke up and had to pull his legs out of the hamper at the end of his bed. "Good morning, D," he said, rubbing the crud from his eyes.

We had a small closet: Aaron and I shared the left half while our father's clothes occupied the right side. Our mother had ironed all our outfits the previous weekend. Now, on Friday, only two items remained on the plastic hangers on our side: our maroon game jerseys. Aaron wore number 15; I wore number 14.

We got up and walked to our bathroom to brush our teeth. We

nudged each other for sink space, competing to see who could keep their toothpaste-spit away from the clean faucet while being elbowed in the stomach. We made weird faces at each other trying to force a laugh so the toothpaste would fall onto our chin or splatter onto the mirror.

WHEN HE WAS YOUNGER, Aaron was ice-skating for the first time at our cousin's birthday party at an indoor rink. Aaron challenged another kid who was an experienced skater to a race. Aaron was in the lead as they neared the first turn, but Aaron forgot one thing: he didn't know how to turn on skates. So he kept flying straight and smashed his head into a wall.

Everyone at the rink turned to the source of the loud bang. Aaron dropped to the ice, landing on his back. He got right up, amazed at not being hurt. He didn't start crying until he noticed the blood coming from his mouth and dripping onto the ice. Our aunt Lisa, seated at a nearby picnic table, cautiously shuffled in her shoes to him as fast as she could. She picked up his two adult front teeth off the ice, her eyebrows raised in shock. Aaron spotted them and let out a piercing scream. Aunt Lisa skittered off the ice back to dry ground and put the teeth in a Ziploc bag, but there was no saving them.

Days later, a dentist fitted Aaron with two prosthetic front teeth. He would always have issues with them. Sometimes he'd bite into an apple and end up losing his teeth. Once his fake teeth were out, it looked like he had a pair of short No. 2 pencils protruding from his gums. To get a rise out of me, he'd bring his head down just above the surface of the table and act like he was using them to write on a sheet of paper. Our abs would hurt from laughing.

THAT WASN'T AARON'S ONLY hard collision as a child. In the summers, when our parents were at work, we loved to build and hammer things. So one day when I was in third grade we went into the woods in our backyard with a few friends and started hammering a piece of wood into a tree with nails. I was holding the board steady and our friend was banging on a nail. As he was hammering, the rusted hammerhead flew backward and smashed into the left side of Aaron's head.

My heart stopped. Aaron dropped to the ground, landing on his butt. I rushed to him and saw he had blood oozing out of his ears and nose.

"Am I going to be okay, D?"

We were both scared. Aaron got up and was able to walk back into our house, where I used paper towels, peroxide, and Q-tips to clean him up.

Many years later, I'm left to wonder: was this the first hit of many that affected my brother's brain?

OUR MOTHER WAS IN the kitchen drinking coffee, smoking a cigarette, and reading the local newspaper. She always looked for sports stories about Aaron and me. She'd cut them out of the *Bristol Press* and tack them onto the bulletin boards above our beds. Aaron and I hated those articles, because they'd fall on our beds in the middle of the night—along with the sharp tacks—but our mom loved looking at them while she ironed.

Aaron and I put on our jerseys and headed to school—our normal routine on game day.

I was so excited, I couldn't get the game against Xavier High School out of my mind all day. I saw Aaron a few times in the hallways and made sure he understood the plays.

"D, I know what I'm doing," he said. "You've told me a hundred times already."

When the final bell rang, Aaron and I went home to take a pregame nap. When my alarm buzzed, we went to the living room and lay on the floor. Our father, who had just returned home from work, was sitting on the sofa. A few hours before kickoff, he always rubbed our feet with his strong hands. With blades of grass on his forearms and with dirt stains on his white tube socks, he dug into our arches to break up the soreness that had built up in our feet from the week of practice.

I walked alone into my room and put on my maroon football pants and long maroon socks. I valued this time. I looked over the play sheet that was wrapped around my left wrist. I wanted to be perfect—especially because it was our season opener and my first varsity game with Aaron. We had both worked so hard for this moment.

Sometimes when I couldn't sleep, I'd roll out of bed, tiptoe to the kitchen door, slide on my shoes, flip on the sidelight, and go outside. Under the amber glow of the crackling driveway light, I'd jump rope with my blue weight vest strapped on. Aaron often woke up and joined me on the driveway.

"Man, you are crazy," he'd say, shaking his head from the top of the steps. But then, seconds later, Aaron would be a few feet away mimicking my motion because we only had one jump rope and had to share.

We'd only stop when our mother came to the door. "What are you doing?" she'd ask. "Come back inside and get to bed."

Before bed every night, we'd see who could do the most push-ups and sit-ups. When one of us would stop, the other would say, "Hey, if you're not working now, someone else is." This was what our father often told us, and we repeated it to each other hundreds of times. We wouldn't quit until our muscles locked up.

Other times before bed we'd compete to see who could plank the longest. We'd hold the position and stare at each other, waiting for the other one to drop. Our entire bodies would shake, but we wouldn't give up until our bodies collapsed to the floor; neither of us ever wanted to lose.

If it was raining, we'd go to our basement and set up cones to run drills. We'd play tag, chasing each other around our pool table to improve our agility and quickness. We'd get on our knees and play tackle football. Other times, we'd run up the stairs from the basement, around the den wall, back down to the basement, and around the pool table like it was a track around a field.

When our father returned home from work, we'd do everything in our power to convince him to join us on the driveway and throw us the football. Aaron and I would push and shove each other, trying to gain position in order to make the catch to impress our dad. I was older and stronger at the time, but Aaron always made it a battle.

We'd play home run derby in our backyard. Once Aaron jacked one of my pitches through our parent's bedroom window. My mother poked her head out of what remained of the shattered glass and asked what the hell happened. Aaron replied, "I finally hit his curveball!"

WHEN IT WAS TIME to return to school, where we would meet up with our team for the ride over to the stadium, our dad followed us to the car. He gave us a hug and a kiss good-bye, and we got in. I rolled down the driver's-side window, and as I backed out of the driveway, he strolled along with us shouting words of encouragement until we reached the end of the driveway. For years, our father had talked about how special the day was going to be when his two boys took the high school playing field together, and now that day had arrived.

Aaron was the only freshman on our team, and I worried that he was nervous. He had as much athletic ability as any of the wide receivers on our team, but he was too young to know it.

I told him that the locker room was quiet on game day—much different than after school on practice days. "When you're getting dressed I want you to envision what you have to do and how you're going to get it done," I said.

I continued. "Before you run with the football tonight, make sure you exaggerate every catch with your eyes. Look at the ball all the way into the tuck. Play hard on every snap."

He nodded.

"Also, the first time I touch the ball, I'm going to score tonight."

He thought I was joking and started laughing.

"I did it last year and I'm going to do it again," I said. "You just watch."

He looked at me as if I were out of my mind.

We parked near the custodian's entrance. We both put our headphones on and listened to our slow-jam mix—Boyz II Men, Jagged Edge—to keep us calm before releasing all of our energy on the field.

Through the cafeteria's glass windows, I saw two yellow school buses lining up with their engines running, waiting to take our team to Muzzy Field, our school's home stadium for football and baseball games.

After a brief team meeting in which we reviewed our first few offensive plays and discussed last-minute adjustments, I grabbed my gear and the game ball, and walked outside. I met Aaron on the sidewalk. He stood about ten yards away and I took a three-step drop and threw him a pass. Aaron exaggerated the catch, tucked it, and tossed the ball back to me.

The team loaded onto the two buses. I took a seat and Aaron sat behind me. Aaron put his hands on my shoulders and squeezed. He whispered into my right ear, "You're going to dominate today."

"You are, too," I said. "We have been waiting a long time for this. Let's both have a day!"

I was always the last one off the bus, so I could watch my teammates in their maroon uniforms stride into the stadium. Aaron waited for me to rise, but I told him to walk out in front of me. I followed closely behind.

As soon as we got off the bus we could smell the burning coals in the concession stand grill. The yellow-jacketed event staff was busy getting the stadium ready for the crowd. I slowed as I neared the front entrance. Every time I reached this spot for our home games, I paused. My dad had played here. My uncles had played here. Even Babe Ruth played here when he was in the minor leagues.

In the old-time locker room, I sat in front of my wooden locker, my eyes closed, visualizing the game ahead. Then I tied the laces on my black Adidas cleats and jogged onto the field. I loved feeling the crunch of the gravel underneath my feet as I ran past home plate, down the third base line before reaching the left field grass, where we warmed up. Aaron was already out on the field.

AARON WAS PHYSICALLY MATURE beyond his age and so skilled that my father often said, "When Aaron develops, he will be special. He's as gifted as they come."

When Aaron was in the seventh grade, he could dunk a basketball. He was an all-around better athlete than I was, and I never possessed his leaping ability. It got to the point where I told Aaron, "Look, if you want to play H-O-R-S-E with me, you can't dunk because I can't." Aaron would nod his head and then we'd go outside to play. But then his very first shot would be a tomahawk jam.

"What did I just tell you?" I'd say.

"Oh yeah," he'd say, then he would smile at me. It was his way of playfully sticking it to his older brother.

We challenged each other often as kids.

One time at a restaurant Aaron boasted he could eat a four-pound burger. He was only twelve at the time, and as his older brother I knew how to push his buttons. "Aaron, there is no way you can eat that entire thing," I said.

Aaron ordered the burger. It filled the entire plate. A few big bites in, his face already covered with ketchup and cheese and beef juice, he looked at me with his mouth full and said, "D, there's no way I can finish this."

We both started laughing.

We gave the leftovers of the burger to our dog, an eighty-pound purebred white German shepherd named UConn. We loved to take a football outside with UConn and try to juke him and run past him on our narrow driveway. He'd nip at our legs and sometimes grab hold of our pants and rip our clothes as we tried to move past. It was a nerve-racking game, but we wanted to replicate what it was like running away from defenders on the football field.

When it was extremely icy outside, we'd go to a local mall to have a catch. In an empty passageway, the football in my hands, I'd get into my quarterback stance and then take a five-step drop. I'd shuffle to the left, to the right, and then forward to replicate escaping an oncoming pass rush. Then I'd yell "Now!" and Aaron, standing twenty feet away and pumping his arms, would either turn back to me to mimic a curl route or turn away from me like he was running a comeback route. A security guard usually asked us to leave after thirty minutes, but that work in the mall was important to us.

AARON AND I STOOD next to each other on the sideline, kickoff against Xavier High seconds away. We spotted a banner that cheerleaders had made and taped onto the green left field fence that read: "The Hernandez Boys #14 & #15."

Xavier received the opening kick and marched down the field for a touchdown, taking a 7–0 lead. Our team trotted onto the field to return the ensuing kickoff. The blockers on our return team all executed their assignments and cleared the path for my ninety-yard touchdown return.

Aaron grabbed me after I said a prayer in the end zone, hugging me. "I can't believe you scored!" he screamed. "You said you were going to do it and you did!"

Later in the first quarter we had the ball at midfield. A receiver brought the play into the huddle from the sideline and I relayed the call to my teammates. I received a shotgun snap and looked at my first progression to the right. But the rush forced me to slide to my left. I looked downfield and spotted Aaron, who was running a drag route across the middle of the field. I hit him in stride and he ran down the right sideline as if his shoelaces were on fire. He dashed into the end zone, his first catch and his first score as a high school player—and my first touchdown pass to my brother. The crowd thundered.

With my hands raised toward the sky, I sprinted after Aaron, who was celebrating with teammates in the end zone. Right before I reached him, I pointed upward and we both jumped as high as we could to chest-bump. My forward momentum knocked Aaron to the ground on his back. Laughing, I helped him up. I pressed my facemask against his and said, "Great play, Aaron! Great play!"

We jogged to the sideline together and shifted our eyes to the bleachers, where our family members and friends were jumping up and down, causing the metal stands to rattle and shake. As we neared the bench, we spotted our father in his maroon fleece. Clapping slowly and nodding his head, he looked directly at us, his lips quivering and tears falling. My mother's arms were around him. Together, Aaron and I pointed up to him. He clenched his right fist, pumped it in the air a few times, and then hugged our mother tight. On this Friday night, under the Muzzy Field lights, his dream—and our dream—came true.

We won the game 44–14. After our head coach addressed the team on the field, I started walking toward the locker room when I noticed my dad in the distance leaning up against the chain-link fence, alone. I ran back to him.

"What's wrong, Dad?" I asked.

"Nothing, D," he said. "I am just so proud. We've come so far.

I'm so thankful for you, for Aaron, and for mom. I love you boys so much."

He whipped the tears of happiness from his cheeks. We hugged and I sprinted to the locker room, where my teammates, and my brother, were dancing and cheering.

We rode the team bus back to Central and then Aaron and I drove home. Our father and mother were waiting for us in the kitchen. Our dad opened his arms and pulled us in—a giant bear hug, holding the two of us so tight and not wanting to let go.

"I am the luckiest father in the world," he said in a whisper. "I love you boys. I could hold you both here forever."

The four of us sat down at the kitchen table and ate cheese-and-pepperoni pizza. My mom told us our father was "crying like a baby" in the stands. Aaron and I mimicked his weeping face, making him laugh along with us.

It was perfect, the four of us together. None of us wanted the night to end.

CHAPTER 5

OCTOBER 7, 2005

Two years had passed since Aaron and I played at Bristol Central together, and now I was standing on the sideline of Rentschler Field in East Hartford, Connecticut, the site of the University of Connecticut football team's home games. Minutes before kickoff, I looked up into the first row of the bleachers and spotted my dad. Knowing he was there always calmed me.

I was a redshirt freshman quarterback and that preseason, Matt Bonislawski had won the starting quarterback position. Early in the second quarter in our Big East conference match-up against Syracuse—the Friday-night game was broadcast on ESPN2—Matt went down with a broken collarbone.

I started taking snaps and throwing the football on the sideline. My father yelled to me, "You got this, D!" I looked up and saw my dad in tears.

I entered the game and helped us win, 26–7.

One month later, I traveled to Newington, Connecticut, during our bye week to watch Aaron, now a junior, play an away game.

During the season, I wrote Aaron short motivational letters that he would tuck into his right sock every Friday night in the locker room. "Every play is an opportunity for you to prove that you are the best player in the country. I love you. Dominate today." When my mother pulled his maroon socks from the dryer later, they would be stained with ink. Aaron always wore those same socks on game day because he was superstitious and felt a part of me was with him.

Aaron didn't know I was coming. With a black splint on my left wrist—I had broken it the week after the Syracuse game against Cincinnati—I sat in the stands for several minutes in silence, not wanting to make him aware of my presence.

In my short time away from home, his body had rapidly filled out. He was a grown man out there, six foot two and 220 pounds. He was the biggest and fastest player warming up on either team.

My father and I sat with Randy Edsall, the head football coach at UConn.

Coach Edsall had already offered Aaron a scholarship the summer before his junior year, and Aaron had verbally accepted. Now Edsall was there to evaluate Aaron in person for the first time.

Minutes before kickoff I walked down out of the visiting bleachers and leaned against a chest-high metal fence that circled the field. "Aaron!" I yelled.

Aaron looked over at me, confused by my presence. He pulled off his helmet and sprinted across the blue track to the fence. "Good luck, I love you," I said. "By the way, Coach Edsall is here. Put on a show tonight."

"Thanks, D," he said. "I love you. I'm so happy you're here."

For the next two hours, Aaron flashed his potential, making play after play after play—one-handed catches, catches in traffic, and standout tackles from his defensive end position. Every time Aaron made a block, it was as if the defender were on roller skates being driven backward. Coach Edsall couldn't sit still. He told my father during the fourth quarter, "I've never seen a high school player this talented in my life."

Aaron finished the game with nine catches for 376 yards and four touchdowns. On that night he set a state high school record for receiving yards in one game, which was also the seventh best in national history.

CHAPTER 6

DECEMBER 2005

I DROVE HOME FROM UCONN to spend my holiday break with my family. I walked through the white front door and the smell of my mother's delicious beef stew filled the entire house.

From the kitchen, I heard a car door slam shut in the driveway. I stepped out of the side door and met my father at his white Chevy Trailblazer. I had a haircut appointment and didn't want my car to be blocked in by his vehicle.

He handed me his keys.

I drove to my hometown barbershop to get a bald fade. Aaron had thin, spiky hair with a widow's peak and I had thick, matted hair—keeping our hair short worked in our favor.

Returning home, I popped the trunk of my car to retrieve my two suitcases and workout gear. It was empty. I found all my bags neatly placed by my bed.

I saw my dad in the kitchen. "You didn't have to bring in all my stuff."

He grinned. "You're not the only one around here with muscles," he said, flexing his little biceps for me. "Come with me to pick up Aaron from basketball practice."

Minutes later my father and I were standing on the Bristol Central basketball court. Watching the end of practice, Aaron did everything with such ease, draining long-range shots and soaring to the rim for dunks on offense and rebounds on defense. "Every time I come back, Aaron gets better and better at everything he does," I said. "He could be an elite college basketball player if he wanted."

OUR DAD HAD A golden rule for us when we played basketball growing up: we were never allowed to surrender an easy layup—even outdoors in the winter. On snow days, we'd shovel the court, but we'd slip and slide over the icy spots. If one of us drove hard to the hoop, we knew we would end up landing in the snowbank behind the basket. We took our dad's directive to heart.

When we got cold, we would run inside, change our clothes, and gulp down a cup of hot chocolate that our mother made for us. Then we'd head back into the freezing afternoon for more basketball. The only thing that interrupted our games was the snowball fights that broke out between us and other kids in the neighborhood. Even though Aaron was the youngest in our group, he could sure fire a snowball.

But we could also argue and fight with each other like brothers. There would be times Aaron and I would be in our basement playing Madden NFL '95 on our Sega Genesis. I would call him "Beaver" and he would call me "Rat tail"—our childhood nicknames for each other. We'd be having fun, talking and horsing around, and then as quickly as a light switch being flipped, Aaron would snap and start hitting me on the wrist with his controller or claw at my face with his nails. I'd run up the cellar stairs and he'd chase me as I yelled for my parents.

Once he calmed down, I'd ask Aaron what happened.

"D, it's like I black out," he'd say with no further explanation.

AFTER PRACTICE WAS OVER, the three of us played a game of P-I-G. Our dad was knocked out first, and then Aaron and I battled away, making shots until our dad told us we had to finish up. Before leaving the gym, Aaron and I made sure to make our last layup—our ritual.

At home, we sat in our normal spots at the dinner table. Mom served the stew and Aaron and I dug in. This was our dad's favorite meal—he loved to take the chunks of beef and put them on the soft buttered Italian bread from Harvest Bakery and make a mini-sandwich—but after a few minutes we noticed he wasn't eating.

"What's wrong, Dennis?" my mother asked.

"I'm not feeling well," he said. "I'm going to lie down."

Aaron and I looked at each other, confused. This wasn't like our dad. He rarely complained about anything and he no longer missed meals—or time—with his family. Something wasn't right.

My mom excused herself from the table to check on him as Aaron and I kept eating. She found him on their bed, lying on his back and staring at the ceiling.

"What is it, Dennis?" she asked. "What's going on?"

"I've got this shooting pain in my stomach. I've never felt pain like this before."

"That's it. I'm taking you to the emergency room."

"There's no need to worry," our father told Aaron and me as he made his way to the front door after our mom went out to start the car.

Still in our seats at the table, Aaron and I didn't understand what was happening to our father.

"He's tough," I said to Aaron. "He'll be alright."

After running a few tests at the hospital, the doctor told my dad he had a strangulated hernia and needed surgery as soon as possible. The procedure was scheduled for the next day, New Year's Eve.

Early the next morning, our father was rolled into the operating room. The surgery was scheduled for two hours, but lasted eight.

Aaron and I went to the hospital that night, but our dad was sleeping.

The next day, January 1, our dad was fully awake and appeared to be his normal self. He looked like he belonged at home. He laughed and cracked jokes with Aaron and me. He complained more about his pinky then his stomach. Back in his football playing days, his right pinky got caught in another player's face mask, bending it to a 45-degree angle. Instead of having surgery, he pulled it straight, but it didn't stay. Eventually it stayed permanently bent. Now in the hospital he asked us to pull it straight. As Aaron yanked, we heard the loud, low rumble of our dad farting, which made everyone in the room laugh and pull their shirts over their noses.

"It was getting too tense in here," he said. "I'll be out in no time. Loosen up."

We spent hours with him, our father nestled between us in the hospital bed, the three of us cuddling. We played checkers, Connect Four, and UNO. That evening a nurse asked him if he was strong enough to go on a short walk down a hallway. He said yes.

Wearing a green gown and hospital socks, with his IV drip bag attached to his left arm, he inched forward alongside the nurse. Aaron and I followed and watched from behind. When the back of his gown swung open to reveal his flat, tan butt, the two of us laughed like it was the most hilarious thing we'd ever witnessed. Our dad turned back to us and winked with a sly smile, which made us laugh even harder.

Later that night, as Aaron and I left the hospital, we thought he looked ready to come home.

THE NEXT AFTERNOON, JANUARY 2, I visited Dad by myself.

His room was dark and silent; no one was visible. I thought I had opened the wrong door, but then I noticed a night lamp shining down on my father, who was shivering underneath his blankets. As I neared him, he lifted his eyelids ever so slightly. He whispered, "Hey, D." I could barely hear his raspy voice.

I leaned over and gently kissed him on his forehead. I had never seen my dad this weak. I knelt so my face was right in front of his.

"What's wrong, Dad?" I asked.

"Not a good day, D, not a good day."

I lowered the bed rail and crawled in next to him, hoping my touch would comfort him. I rubbed his dark eyebrows and hair, trying to soothe him.

"Not a good day, D," he said again.

I didn't want my father to see my worry, so I closed my eyes and remained silent.

"Are you okay?" he asked.

I couldn't answer. Silently, I told myself, *Be strong. Be strong. He needs my strength.*

A few minutes later, he said, "D, I need to get some rest."

I gave him one last squeeze in bed, then asked the nurse for another blanket. I tucked it tightly around him. "Hang in there, Dad," I said. "Everything will be better soon."

I bent over and kissed him again on his forehead.

"I love you, Dad," I said.

With his eyes shut, in a barely audible voice, he said, "I love you, DJ."

I have to be strong for my mother.

I have to be strong for my brother.

I have to be a man.

At the lowest elevation of our hill, I parked my car. Flipping on my flashers, my forehead resting on the steering wheel, I was shredded by the thought of life without my father.

As I walked in the house, my mother was getting ready to leave for the hospital. Aaron already had left for his basketball game that night. Neither of them knew.

About ten minutes later, my uncle Vito picked me up and drove me to Aaron's basketball game. Sitting in his car, I stared at the dashboard. He spoke to me, but the words didn't register.

I thought Aaron's game would distract me from my father—I loved witnessing Aaron's growth as an athlete. Yet as soon as the game started, I knew that wasn't going to happen. My mind remained on my father. On the court, Aaron, for the first time, appeared winded in an athletic contest. When the other team took foul shots, Aaron—hands on knees, bent over—looked directly at me. Aaron scored 29 points, quietly.

THE FOLLOWING DAY, THE doctors informed my mother that our father was in toxic shock. His organs were shutting down.

Early in the morning of January 5, our mother woke us up. She had large purple rings around her eyes. Her hair was frizzy—sticking out in every direction. She looked like she hadn't slept in days.

"Dad had to go to the ICU last night," she said.

"What's the ICU mean?" I asked.

"It's the intensive care unit," she said. "It's where patients go when they are very sick. The patients who need to be monitored very closely. He isn't doing well. I think that you guys should get some rest today and go see him tomorrow."

Early the next morning, our mom called Bristol Hospital and asked if they could transfer our dad to Hartford Hospital, where she thought he could receive advanced treatment.

"He's not doing well," the nurse said. "You should come to the hospital as soon as you can."

In the hallway outside our dad's room, we put on latex gloves, a yellow gown, and a white mask to cover our faces. We entered and I used my right hand to slide the curtain to the side. There was an IV bag dripping fluid into his left arm and a ventilator tube coming out of his mouth, which kept him breathing.

I leaned in close to his ear and told him to hang in there, to keep fighting. I told him I was so proud of the changes he had made in his life to become the best father I ever could have wished for.

My mother was on the other side of the bed, rubbing his arm. Aaron stood behind her, paralyzed.

After about an hour of staring at his closed eyelids, the doctor recommended that we return home to get some rest. He said there was nothing we could do at this time and he would contact us later with an update.

We returned to the house. But just as Aaron and I placed our heads down on our pillows, our mother opened the door to our room.

"DJ, Aaron, get up now!" she screamed. "We have to get back to the hospital now!"

Gripping the steering wheel so hard that the veins in her hands bulged, my mother drove like lightning for five minutes back to Bristol Hospital. Aaron, in the backseat, started to sob. Then we all did.

When we reached the waiting room outside the ICU, a dozen family members had already gathered. A few were kneeling together, circled in prayer. Others were on their feet, crying. Our dad's sister sat in her wheelchair with her face in her hands, yelling, "He's not going to make it! He's not going to make it!"

We continued past them to my father's room. I threw the curtains off to the side in time to see the doctor yell "Clear!" as he held the two defibrillator paddles to our dad's chest.

The three of us stood with our hands clasped, five feet in front of the footboard, watching helplessly, in horror. The doctor again pressed the paddles on our dad, causing his chest to jump and his legs and toes to kick toward us.

"Clear!"

They shocked him again.

"Clear!"

They shocked him again.

Aaron squeezed my left hand tighter. "Please, DJ, please, DJ, help him!"

I felt my mom begin to fall. I grabbed both of them harder.

"Everything is going to be okay," I said to them. "Keep fighting, Dad!" I shouted to my father. "Keep fighting!"

"Come on, Dad!" Aaron yelled.

The doctor paused, the paddles held up in midair. There was no response. Only the steady *beeeeeeeeeeeeeeeep* from the heart monitor. Flatline.

Time of death: 12:05 p.m., January 6, 2006. He was forty-nine years old.

The three of us walked forward to our leader. I put my left ear on his chest, hoping to hear one more beat. Aaron's head rested on the other side of his belly. Our tears pooled in his belly button.

Our mother kissed him on his forehead and rubbed his thick black hair. After about twenty minutes, I finally let go.

I softly told Aaron that when he was ready we needed to leave. Aaron kept his arms around our dad, unwilling to move. I hugged Aaron. He didn't want to let go. "It's time," I whispered. After several minutes, Aaron released his grasp.

That night, after family and friends had left our house, Aaron and I went to our room. In the dark, we whispered to each other from our beds about never hearing Dad's voice again. I slid into Aaron's bed. I held my cell phone between us and we listened to our dad's voice mail greeting over and over and over.

CHAPTER 7

JANUARY 2006

THE LINE STRETCHED OUT the door of the funeral home, onto and around the spacious front porch, through the parking lot, and up Lincoln Avenue for a quarter of a mile. The director estimated that more than one thousand people came to our father's visitation on January 8.

My mother, Aaron, and I stood next to the dark wooden casket, waiting to greet everyone after they said their final good-byes to Dennis Hernandez. I was in a black suit and one of my father's favorite black-and-yellow ties. To my right, my mother, in a long black dress and sweater, wept during the four-hour wake. "He's at peace now. He's at peace now," she repeatedly said.

To my left was Aaron, outfitted in a gray pinstripe suit—the first suit he'd ever worn. Our dad never had the chance to teach him how to tie a tie, so that morning I assisted Aaron, putting another one of our father's ties into a single Windsor for him.

All afternoon, Aaron stood still and silent, looking straight ahead, as if his eyes were locked on to something far in the distance, past everyone in the room, past the walls of the chapel in the funeral home. He never cried.

Once the room was empty, I shut the doors, so the four of us could be together one last time. Aaron and I took a knee in the pew in front of the open casket, holding hands. Our mother stood behind us, caressing our shoulders. After several minutes, my mother and I kissed my father on the forehead. Aaron couldn't bear the sight of our father; Aaron tapped him on his hands and looked away so he wouldn't see his face.

That night the three of us slept together in my parents' bed. My father used two pillows; Aaron and I each buried our heads into one of them, trying to hold on to his scent. Several times during the night our mother ran to the bathroom to vomit. After the first time, we followed her in, rubbing her back and holding her hair as she knelt over the bowl.

THE FUNERAL SERVICE WAS the next morning at St. Joseph's Church in Bristol. The three of us sat in the front wooden pew. Aaron's chest was out, his shoulders back, and his eyes focused forward, rarely moving right or left. Holding my left hand, he felt the jerk from my body when I cried, which caused him to squeeze my hand tighter. Midway through the funeral, my mother leaned in to us and asked us if we wanted to say any words about our father. Aaron closed his eyes and shook his head. I whispered, "I can't, Mom. There's no way I can talk right now."

Once the service concluded, we stood up from the pew and wiggled our legs to loosen up. We didn't know what to do next. The funeral director waved to us and we followed our mom down the center aisle outside to a black town car waiting for us at the curb. I looked out the back window as we began the drive to the cemetery and saw a long trail of cars in the procession, their hazard lights all flashing. A police cruiser led the way.

At the grave site, we took our seats about eight feet from where the casket would soon be lowered. As soon as the short ceremony began, I grabbed Aaron's thigh to let him know I was there for him.

I eventually lifted my eyes from my lap and saw mourners piling flowers on the casket. The three of us waited in our chairs, shivering in the cold, for every last person to lay their rose. Then we slowly placed our own roses onto the casket before returning to our car.

A large group gathered at Nuchie's, a local restaurant, to celebrate our father. I didn't understand why people were laughing as they shared stories over lunch. Only one hour earlier, we had left our father to be buried into the frozen ground. I turned to my mom and whispered, "Why are they talking?"

"People are telling good stories about your dad," my mom said softly. "They're sharing stories about the amazing man he was."

"THE GOOD DAYS WITH him were so exciting," she told me in the days after his death. "He was so nice, he was funny, he was beautiful, he was a great dancer, and he made me feel special. He also was a big football star. He had a great smile and muscles. He became a great father. There was so much about the man I loved."

But she also hated him at times. "On our wedding night, I caught your dad going to the bathroom and snorting cocaine," she said. "We got into a fight and your father ripped off my wedding ring, picked up a hammer, and smashed it, bending the ring and dislodging the diamonds. The next morning he apologized. 'It won't happen again,' he told me."

She had held in a lot. "There were two sides to your father—when he was clean of drugs and when he wasn't," she said. "The night after Aaron was born, your father didn't even show up at the hospital. He was so fucked-up, he left you with someone and went out to party. He wasn't there for Aaron and me that night.

"I went through a lot of shit with him, and I'm sorry, because I took it out on you kids. I look back now and think, *How the hell did we ever survive that shit?*"

IN THE CAR, MY mother asked Aaron if he wanted to play in his high school basketball game that evening.

"What do you think Dad would have wanted me to do?" Aaron asked.

"He would have said, 'Keep moving forward,'" my mom said. I agreed.

"But who will I hand the ball to if I score my one thousandth point tonight? It was supposed to be Dad."

When we got home, Aaron called our uncle David, our father's twin brother, who was battling liver cancer but was able to attend the funeral. Aaron asked him if he could come to the game and accept the ball. "I wouldn't miss it for the world," Uncle David said.

A few hours later, my mother and I entered the front glass doors at Bristol Central. As we were walking through the hallways, one person after the next approached and offered condolences—almost like another receiving line leading into the gymnasium. When we entered, the crowd fell silent; suddenly the only sounds were the bouncing of the balls and squeaks of the players' shoes during warm-ups. We felt every set of eyes turn to us.

I spotted Aaron dribbling a basketball in the hallway outside the locker room, preparing to enter the gym for pregame warm-ups. I went to him, wished him good luck, and asked how he was feeling.

"I'm doing alright, D," he said.

Returning to my seat, I thought how different this night was going to be from when I had scored my 1,000th point three years earlier, when I had handed my milestone ball to my father. If he had been here tonight, he would be sitting next to me chewing on his right thumb, commenting on the game and Aaron's play. He would have been the happiest guy in the gym.

Before tip-off, the public address announcer asked everyone to stand and remove their hats for a moment of silence for our father. I didn't want to close my eyes because they had been shut from crying for most of the last two days. From the bleachers, I looked at my brother six rows down on the wooden court. His eyes were closed, his hands were clasped behind his back, and he was gently swaying left to right.

Minutes into the game, Aaron had the ball on a fast break. He soared into the air for a rim-rattling dunk. The packed gym erupted. A few possessions later, Aaron slashed to the basket for a right-handed layup—his 1,000th career point. The scorekeeper buzzed the horn as the ball dropped through the net.

The officials whistled to stop the game and asked Aaron to come to midcourt, where they acknowledged his accomplishment and presented him with the ball. Receiving a standing ovation, Aaron jogged up into the bleachers toward our uncle and handed him the ball before the action resumed.

A few days later, preparing to drive back to college to begin my spring semester, I talked to Aaron. "If you need anything, I'm only forty-five minutes away," I said. "Dad would have wanted you to remain focused and keep working hard. Mom might need your help more around the house. After basketball season is over, maybe we can plan something and you can come spend time with me?"

"That would be amazing, D," he said.

Aaron sat on the front steps, watching me drive away.

CHAPTER 8

FEBRUARY 2006

THE SECOND WEEK OF February I returned to Bristol for my father's birthday. On the way, I stopped at Family Dollar and bought his favorite candy, Red Hot Dollars. I planned to leave the box on his headstone.

I asked Aaron to come with me to the cemetery, but he insisted on staying home. "I'm not ready, D," he said. "I'm not going until I win a Super Bowl."

It was too early to press him, so I went to the burial site by myself. Standing on the hardened dirt, I bent down, wished my father a happy fiftieth, and placed his candy next to a birthday card my mother had left the day before. The headstone wasn't in place yet.

Before going back to my dorm the next day, Aaron caught me off guard with a question as I was exiting the house. "D, do you think I'm good enough to play somewhere besides UConn?" he asked.

"You're good enough to play wherever you want. You being committed to UConn is a huge deal for our program and everyone is excited about you coming. You're going to dominate when you get to campus. I can't wait to play with you again."

Two months later, I received a phone call from Aaron. "I don't want you to be upset," he said, "but I am going to visit the University of Florida."

"Have you told Coach Edsall yet?"

"No," he said.

"You need to tell him before you go," I said. "Dad would be pissed at you if you visited Florida behind Coach Edsall's back and you know that."

"Please don't say anything, D," he said.

"Aaron, it's not my place to say anything, but you need to tell him," I said. "And do not commit to Florida during your trip. Wait until you're home so we can discuss everything."

I hung up the phone and called my mother.

"What's going on with Aaron?" I asked. "He's visiting Florida?"

"He's excited about going," she said. "I called one of his old youth coaches and asked him to go on the trip with him. I need a man's perspective now that your dad is not here. He knows more about football and recruiting than I do."

A week later Aaron and his youth coach, Tom Wagman, flew to Gainesville for Aaron's unofficial visit. "We were sitting on the plane and we made a pros-and-cons list on a sheet of paper to compare all the colleges that were recruiting Aaron," Tom told me. "I looked over at Aaron and said, 'Do not make your decision until we return home.' I reminded him that he was committed to UConn. Before we got off the plane I said it again."

Aaron and Tom drove to the Gators football facility, where they spotted hundreds of Winnebagos parked in the lots in anticipation of the spring game the following day. Fans covered in orange-and-blue gear walked near the stadium.

They were greeted by two assistant coaches and taken to watch practice. Hundreds ringed the practice field. "The atmosphere was electric," Tom said. Afterward, the coaches took them to Ben Hill Griffin Stadium—the Gators home field, known as "The Swamp."

Once they arrived at the Gator Walk, the coaches described how on game day, when the bus doors open, thousands of fans line the brick walkway to cheer and snap photos of the players as they descend from the buses, the fans reaching over the ropes to slap the players' hands.

Aaron stepped out of the tunnel and looked at the steep bleachers and at the orange walls as music blared from the speakers. It was the biggest stadium Aaron had ever entered, and he couldn't stop smiling.

He bent down and skimmed his hands over the short-cut grass field. "Is this really grass?" Aaron asked, accustomed to the turf we played on in high school. The Florida coaches laughed and confirmed that the grass was real.

After touring the facilities, Aaron met with quarterback Tim Tebow, who told Aaron how excited he was that Aaron was considering Florida. Aaron immediately liked him.

Aaron wanted to be wearing the school colors for the game, so the next morning Tom took him shopping for a pair of blue shoes. He wanted to look like he was a part of the team.

Aaron watched the game from the sideline. Afterward he met with the entire Gator coaching staff in the football facility. The coaches were sitting around a long table and Aaron took a seat with them.

"Well, how did you like that?" Urban Meyer, the head coach, asked.

Aaron stood up from his seat and blurted out, "I am coming here."

The Florida coaches high-fived each other and hugged Aaron.

But Aaron's youth coach, Tom, was shocked. "No, no, no," he said. "Urban, it's not happening like this. Aaron has to make two phone calls right now. The minute we leave here, it's going to be on the Internet and everywhere. He has to call his mom and he has to call Randy Edsall at UConn."

My phone started to ring as I was driving back from Hanover,

New Hampshire, where I had watched the Dartmouth College spring game.

"Hey, D," Aaron said. "I just want you to know that I committed to Florida."

"Did you tell Coach Edsall?"

"No," he said.

"What did I tell you, Aaron?" I said, raising my voice. "You're a fucking idiot. I can't believe you did this, Aaron."

Just then my flip phone began vibrating and ringing. I looked at who was calling: Coach Edsall. I ignored the incoming call and remained on the line with Aaron. Edsall phoned a second time. "Edsall is blowing up my phone right now," I said. "You need to call him, Aaron."

"What should I say to him?"

"That's your problem now," I said.

Coach Edsall called a third time. I was finished speaking with Aaron, so I answered. "DJ, what is going on with Aaron?" Edsall said, his voice frantic. "What the hell is going on?"

"Coach," I said, "I'm still trying to figure this all out myself."

I was pissed. I didn't care that Aaron wanted to check out Florida. I was disappointed with how quickly everything transpired considering the limited amount of information he had gathered. He could have gone to virtually any top program in the country and I wanted him to put some thought into his decision.

In Florida, Aaron paced nervously as he dialed Edsall's number. Edsall answered the phone and Aaron informed him of his decision.

"Edsall chewed him a new ass, up and down," the youth coach said. "Aaron took the phone and held it away from his ear because Edsall was screaming so loud."

Then Aaron called our mother. "Mom, I like it here," he said. "I committed to Florida and I'm happy about that. But I'm also upset because it seems like I let Coach Edsall down."

Aaron handed the phone to Coach Meyer, who spoke to my mother for a few minutes, assuring her that Aaron would be in good hands.

After leaving the facility, Aaron and his youth coach went to celebrate by getting ice cream. As Aaron dug for his second spoonful, a fan approached. "You're Aaron Hernandez," the fan said. "You just committed here!"

On the way back to the hotel, several local reporters called Aaron's cell phone, asking for a comment. A few other reporters showed up at the hotel, where they interviewed Aaron outside the lobby.

Once the media left, Aaron relaxed in his room. "This is the best place for me," Aaron said to his youth coach. "It's where I have to go to get to the NFL. And I'll have a chance to win a national championship here."

When they returned to Connecticut a few days later, Aaron changed his mind. "I think I want to go to UConn," Aaron told his youth coach.

"I will back you on whatever you want to do," the youth coach said. "You think about everything that happened. You think about it."

Aaron wavered again: he was going to Florida.

I RETURNED TO UCONN, feeling like I had done something wrong. I went to Coach Edsall's office to speak with him. I didn't want this to fester.

"I'm so sorry, Coach," I said. "I hope my brother's decision doesn't affect me in any way."

"You had nothing to do with this," he said. "It's not your fault. I'm just blown away by his decision. Aaron doesn't know much about Florida. I can't believe he didn't talk to me first."

"I know, Coach," I said, shaking my head. "Neither can I."

CHAPTER 9

JULY 2006

THAT SUMMER, I STAYED at UConn, working out with the team. I called home a few times a week, checking in on my mom and Aaron. But even that was hard, because the phone calls triggered memories of my dad. He had always answered when he was home, often picking up halfway through the first ring. With Dad no longer present, my mom now answered the phone and she always sounded tired, like she hadn't slept in days.

One July weekend I went home to visit. I noticed a change in the house as soon as I opened the side door. I knew that Aaron didn't have a game and my mother had finished work for the day, but no one was in the kitchen and the lights were off. I walked across the worn green rug into the living room. The television was off and the sectional couch looked as if it hadn't been touched in months. The throw pillows had no body-weight imprints on them and the remotes were side by side on the ottoman.

I went to my childhood bedroom. I turned on the light; the blue blinds were pulled down to the window ledge above my old bed. Wrinkled clothes were stacked up on the ironing board.

In the old days, Aaron would sometimes jump out from around a corner and yell "Ahhhhh!" to surprise me. Today no one was there.

I opened the old wooden doors to my father's side of the closet. His clothes were still there, untouched since the day he died. I grabbed the right sleeve to his beloved maroon fleece and lifted it to my nose. His scent was lost, overtaken by the constant smoke coming from my mother's burning cigarette.

I walked into my parents' room. It was dark, the bed wasn't made, and the nineteen-inch TV cast its glow over my mom, lying on her side under the covers. It was the middle of the afternoon and she was sound asleep.

Her black nightstand was covered with balled tissues, and the ashtray—which she always dumped out—overflowed with a mound of crushed cigarette butts. I gave her a kiss on her head before she woke up and let out a slow, "Heyyyyy."

She turned on her bedside lamp and stood up. I was startled. "Mom, are you okay?" I asked. "You look exhausted. You are so skinny. Are you eating?"

"D, I've lost thirty-five pounds," she said. "I'm down to one hundred." Her pants didn't fit and her neck was thinner.

"It's like I have a nervous energy constantly traveling through my body," she said. "I can't make it stop."

The first few months after my father's passing, I, too, had trouble eating. My weight had dropped from 212 pounds to 182. I vomited often. Almost every time I put food near my mouth, I experienced a gagging sensation. For breakfast I'd go to the dining hall and try to keep down a banana. But now, five months after the funeral, my appetite had returned and my weight was back up to 205.

"I'm so sorry, Mom," I said. "Do you know where Aaron is?"

"He's either working out or over at Tanya's," she said.

Growing up, back when Aaron was in diapers, my father's older sister, Ruthie, and her daughter Tanya used to babysit us. I remember sitting under the kitchen table next to my aunt's leg as three Rottweilers roamed around the kitchen floor. They terrified us. Every now and then, my aunt would drop one of her Bingo markers on the ground and Aaron and I would stamp each other with it. As Aaron grew older, his relationship with Tanya strengthened.

Aunt Ruthie and Tanya would welcome anyone with a pulse into their house—drug dealers, drug users, even convicted felons. At times our dad would stay there all night playing dominoes and drinking with the guys. Aaron and I would be at the kitchen table playing board games with our cousins and aunts until our mother said it was time to leave. When our mother gave us the ten-minute warning, we would begin giving our family members at the table hugs and kisses before going downstairs to say good-bye to everyone else. Walking down the steps, we passed through clouds of smoke.

"The boys and I are leaving in five minutes," she'd tell our dad. If he wanted to stay and finish his game, our mother would say, "Find a ride. We are leaving."

On the car ride home, she would be pissed that he didn't come with us. "I fucking hate going over there," she told us. "In that house there's no rules, no structure, and they let people do whatever the hell they want."

The next morning, we would have a bowl of Fruity Pebbles for breakfast and then make our way to the living room. My mother, Aaron, and I would be watching television and our father would spend the entire day snoring in his bed. "That son of a bitch," our mom would say. "I hate when he fucking goes over there."

Years later, it was at Tanya's where Aaron would be introduced to Ernest "Bo" Wallace.

AARON'S DAILY ROUTINE CONTINUED as before. He seemed happy and rarely expressed any hurt, pain, or depression that he might have been experiencing. My mother would ask him if he was okay, and he'd respond with one word: "Yeah." Unlike our mom and me, he was gaining weight rather than losing it.

Whenever I asked "How are you doing?" he'd reply "I'm fine, D" and change the subject. He was immersed in working out.

One night he was running hills with a weight vest on with one of his teammates. The other kid passed out from the exertion, and as Aaron carried him home, he told him, "I am going to be the best tight end in the NFL someday, you watch. I work harder than anyone else."

When Aaron wasn't training, he would usually spend time with Tanya and Tanya's husband, Jeff, who in a short period had become Aaron's closest friend in Bristol. Jeff taught him how to drive and how to fish. Aaron asked me to join them one morning when I was home during my summer break.

Right away, as we stood close together with our lines cast in a still pond deep in the woods, I noticed they had a great rapport. Their conversation was smooth and effortless.

In September of Aaron's junior year, he made his official visit to Florida. Aaron invited his high school coach and Jeff to come along with my mother. One night, after Aaron had gone off with his host and several other Florida football players, my mother and Jeff explored campus together. They eventually stopped for pizza, then returned to the hotel with a six-pack of cold beer. They talked for hours.

BACK IN BRISTOL, JEFF and my mother would cheer on Aaron at his basketball games. Both smokers, they often went outside together for a cigarette. Jeff asked my mother if she would be interested in grabbing drinks one night.

A few nights later, they met in the school parking lot. As Jeff closed the passenger door to my mom's silver Nissan, Tanya pulled up in front with her brights on. She jumped out of her car and began shouting at Jeff and my mom, accusing them of having an affair. My mom told Jeff he should get out of the car and go with Tanya.

As Jeff stepped out, my mom said, "Tanya, we're not doing anything wrong."

My mom drove off by herself. Tanya followed closely, flashing her high beams and honking her horn. My mother took a left into the gas station at the bottom of the hill. Tanya parked behind her and told Jeff to get out of the car. "You're fucking my husband!" Tanya yelled to my mom. "I can't believe you're fucking my husband!"

"Tanya," my mom said, "we didn't do anything. We were going to have a drink."

Tanya peeled off. Jeff got into my mom's car a second time and she took him back to the school's parking lot to retrieve his white hoopty. They decided to go get a drink like they had planned.

Tanya went home and immediately marched across the street to the youth football field, where Aaron was watching a practice.

"Your mother is fucking my husband!" she yelled loud enough for everyone in the crowd to hear.

Aaron was stunned.

THAT NIGHT I WAS lying in my hotel bedroom in Bloomington, Indiana. The next afternoon I would be making my fifth career start at quarterback against the Hoosiers. The room was dark, the TV was on, and my roommate, another quarterback, was napping in his bed on the other side of the room.

My phone vibrated. I answered.

"I can't take this anymore, D," Aaron said.

"Calm down," I said. "Please tell me what's wrong?"

"Mom ruined our family," he said.

"Aaron, where are you?"

"I'm over Tanya's now," he said.

"Let me call Mom and I'll call you right back."

I dialed my mother's number. "Mom, how could you?"

"Everything is being blown out of proportion, D," she said. "I didn't do anything wrong. I don't know why everyone is acting like this."

I called Aaron back and told him I had to attend a team meeting.

As I sat with the other quarterbacks, my mind wasn't on Indiana; all I could concentrate on was what was happening to my family in Bristol.

After the meeting, I sat on a step in the hotel stairwell and phoned Aaron. He was crying and saying that our mother wasn't answering her cell phone anymore.

It was getting close to bed check, so I returned to my room, still talking to Aaron. I was usually in bed asleep by now, but I didn't want to leave him alone like this. I buried my head under my pillow and whispered, not wanting to wake up my roommate. I fell asleep with Aaron on the other end of the phone.

The next day I played the worst game of my career. I was 5 of 13 for 27 yards, with two interceptions, and lost a fumble going into the end zone. I was a sleeping quarterback, no energy. I was relieved we won, 14–7.

The next day, back at UConn, I walked into the film room to review the game tape with my position group. Just before the projector bulb warmed up and shined out onto the white screen, Coach Edsall entered the room.

"We have to play better at the quarterback position and we need more consistency," he said. "We're going to make a change this upcoming week. DJ, you're going to be the backup."

"Okay," I said. "It's a business. You have to do what you have to do."

I was shocked that those words even came out of my mouth. It caught both Edsall and my quarterback coach by surprise. Edsall asked me if everything was okay.

"Yep," I said.

Before the Indiana game, being the starting quarterback for the Huskies was everything I had ever worked for. But over the next few weeks, Edsall could tell I wasn't focused because of my poor play from practice to practice. He finally asked me to come up to his office.

As soon as I sat down in front of his desk, he rose from his chair and shut both of his office doors behind me. Right then I knew this was going to be a serious conversation.

"DJ, I need to know what's going on," he said. "You've been a leader for us, but I've noticed something hasn't been right for a while."

He looked at me in silence, waiting for me to respond. I met his stare, saying nothing, shaking my head. I didn't want to open up about my family. I was ashamed of what my mother had done; I thought it made my entire family look bad.

Finally, Edsall spoke again. "DJ, I don't want to do this, but if things don't change soon, we are going to move you down to the scout team because we aren't getting anything out of you. If you don't let anyone in, no one can help you."

Edsall sat there patiently, waiting for me to say something, anything.

"DJ," he said softly, "I'm here for you."

"Coach, I lost my family," I said, with my voice cracking. "I have nothing. My father died, my brother is going to Florida, and my mother took my cousin's husband. My family will never be the same."

Trying to keep it together, I explained to him that I hadn't spoken to my mother in months, since the night before the Indiana game. I told him how much I hated my life.

Edsall got out of his leather chair and gave me a fatherly hug. He left the room for a minute and then returned with my position coach. "Anything you need, just tell us," Edsall said. "We'll always be here for you."

I walked out of his office ready to move forward. I felt like I had a family again—my football family.

IT WAS WORSE FOR Aaron. Four days after the Indiana game, our grandmother had told Aaron, who was staying with Tanya, to call our mother.

"Aaron, I didn't do anything wrong," my mother said, referring to her night out with Jeff. "I'm sorry. I didn't mean to hurt you."

Tanya had started telling Aaron that our mother and Jeff had likely been seeing each other when our father was alive. Tanya wouldn't even let Aaron say my mother's name; Jeff would soon move out of Tanya's house. "It was like Aaron was being brainwashed to hate me," my mother told me later. "There was no truth to what Tanya was telling him. I was sick of their shit and the things they were allowing him to do over there."

My mom finally called Tanya.

"A bartender just called me at work telling me you brought my sixteen-year-old son into their bar and slipped him drinks," she said. "It stops now!"

Tanya replied, "I'm his mother now," and hung up.

Their tension grew as time passed. In November, Jeff moved out of Tanya's house. In December, my mother sat Aaron down and explained that she was going to start dating Jeff.

After losing our dad, Aaron now felt like he had lost everything—me to college, our father to death, and now our mother to Jeff.

CHAPTER 10

OCTOBER 2006

On october 21, bristol central played Maloney High School at Muzzy Field. I returned to watch Aaron play for the first time during his senior season.

With less than two minutes remaining in the fourth quarter, Bristol trailed, 27–26. I couldn't take my eyes off my brother as the offense moved down the field. On the next snap, Aaron fired out of his three-point stance to engage in a block. His helmet collided with a linebacker's helmet. Aaron's body went limp, falling to the ground—first his butt, then his back, and then the back of his maroon helmet.

His body remained motionless as trainers and coaches ran out onto the field to gather around him. I looked up to the top of the press box where Bristol's offense coordinator sat, asking for an update. He shook his head, because he didn't have one yet.

Finally, the trainer guided Aaron upright before Aaron took his helmet off. When Aaron got to his feet, the crowd clapped. The trainer and his head coach helped him off the field.

I saw Aaron smile as he walked and talked. But then his body language shifted when his coach said, "Aaron, you are done for the night."

"I am fine, Coach," Aaron said. "I am ready to go back in."

I could tell something was wrong so I ran out of the stands to ask Aaron if he was okay. He said his coach wouldn't let him play anymore. "I need to be out there," Aaron told me. "I need to be out there with my team."

"Calm down," I said. "You don't need to be out there right now."

"I'm fine, I have to be in there," he stated. "My team needs me."

Determined to reenter the game, Aaron started going up to his teammates and asking if he could borrow a helmet.

"Let me wear your helmet," he said to each in turn.

I was confused. I looked back to the top of the press box and asked my old offensive coordinator if Aaron was going to return to play. "No," he said. "Your brother was knocked out cold. He's done."

Aaron remained sidelined for the rest of the game as he watched his team lose. He felt like he let his teammates down.

My mother drove Aaron to the hospital, where doctors confirmed he had a concussion. After the exam, Aaron told our mom to take him to Tanya's. "There was no telling Aaron the word *no,*" she told me. "Aaron no longer had respect for me. He was done listening to me."

AT THE CLOSE OF the season, Aaron was invited to play in the U.S. Army All-American Bowl in San Antonio, Texas. Aaron had finished his high school career with 3,677 receiving yards and 47 touchdowns—both state records. And his 180.7 receiving yards per game over his high school career was a national record. He was a two-time All-American and a two-time state player of the year.

My entire family met Aaron in San Antonio. This was the first time I witnessed how much hatred Aaron had developed for our mother. I could tell he was still seething from her decision to be with Jeff. After the game Aaron walked over to the stands and was nice to everyone, but he wouldn't acknowledge our mother. When she approached him, he said, "I don't talk to sluts or whores."

We flew from San Antonio to Gainesville, Florida, to move Aaron into his college dorm. He had finished high school a semester early so he could participate in spring football practice with the Gators.

In our hotel room we watched Florida beat Ohio State for the national championship. Sitting on our beds, Aaron finally asked me how he played in the All-Star game. "You didn't look focused," I said. "You were all over the place. You better pick it up because if you play like that at Florida, you're not going to be playing much."

The next morning we, along with our mother, drove to Walmart and filled a few carts with items Aaron would need in his dorm room. Our mother was trying to do anything to connect with Aaron, but he remained distant.

I couldn't wait to get away from the arguing and resume my life at UConn.

CHAPTER 11

JUNE 2007

I GAVE AARON SPACE, ALLOWING him to settle into his new environment in Gainesville. After a few weeks, I called him to see how he was adapting to college life.

"How is everything going?" I asked.

"It's good," he said. He talked about the weather and how much he enjoyed the cool breeze at night. He spoke about how much he was studying his playbook and the amount of film he was watching. He thought he would have a good chance of playing as a true freshman.

At the end of Aaron's first semester of college, we both returned home for his high school graduation. When I pulled into our driveway, I found Aaron in our backyard with a few of his high school friends. Aaron was still angry with our mom, but he met some of his old buddies at our backyard pool. He spoke with a thick southern accent—thicker than some of my teammates who were from Georgia and Florida.

I thought Aaron was messing with me, but he carried on like it was his normal way of speaking. His drawl was so heavy that at times I couldn't understand him.

"You know you grew up in Connecticut, right?" I finally said.

I pointed down to his new "860/Connecticut" tattoo on his right shin to remind him. Was this Aaron trying to fit in at Florida?

One afternoon the two of us worked out together and then went to our mother's house to hang out by the pool. Neither of us was staying there—I was at my girlfriend's house and Aaron was at Tanya's—but it was good to be back home. Our mom was at work and Aaron's friends weren't in sight, so it was just the two of us, which meant Aaron didn't have to try so hard to fit in. He could be himself. He dropped the accent.

He sounded thrilled about Florida and everyone there. He loved his teammates and told me that he often texted his coaches late at night when he was working out or running up and down the stadium steps. "I will be the greatest and I will not let you down," he'd tell them.

Then he told me about a girl he was spending time with. He had met Alyssa in a class and he said that she had a wonderful, caring heart. I was surprised, because growing up he rarely talked about girls he was interested in. I knew he'd dated a girl named Shayanna in high school, but they separated shortly after he moved to Florida because of the distance. Aaron said Alyssa made him laugh.

As we sat on the edge of the pool with our feet in the water, Aaron said, "I'll give her a call right now and put her on speaker. She's hilarious."

He was right—she was funny and quick with comebacks. He seemed really happy.

"HE WAS VERY CLOSED off, but the more he was around he just became himself," Alyssa told me later.

"Aaron got this random idea to get a dog," she said. He couldn't have a dog in his dorm, so he made a deal with one of Alyssa's roommates to keep the dog at their place, but he had to take care of it.

"He would go to practice and then bring us food for dinner, and we would watch a movie. We became best friends. One day I came home, and he was moving all of his stuff in."

Alyssa's roommates liked to smoke marijuana, and Aaron would join them. Alyssa told him, "I don't think you're supposed to be smoking." And he said, "Whatever, I do it all the time."

"He was very insecure about his schoolwork," she said. "He used to brag about being an honor student in high school and then when it came to writing his papers he'd say, 'Oh I got a tutor for that.'" She encouraged him to write his next paper without help, which he took as a challenge, so he did it. "I thought it was very well written," she said. "He had taken the time to put the effort into it. Aaron was so proud of it."

Then one of her roommates got a hold of it. "She kind of mocked him. I could see on Aaron's face how much it hurt him, like, 'This is why I don't try.'

"He didn't like to be in vulnerable positions," she said. "He didn't show that side of himself. Even though he came off as confident, he didn't really like people to know him."

Aaron often used her computer. One night she came home late and discovered the Internet search history had been deleted. She thought that was strange, because she didn't believe Aaron had anything to hide. She asked Aaron why he erased what he had been looking at.

"I don't want you to see the porn," Aaron joked.

Alyssa figured out how to undo what he had deleted. "I saw that he was looking at a gay porn site," she said. "It hurt me at the time because I was absolutely in love with him, but at first I didn't question him about it because I thought it wasn't my place."

Then one afternoon she gave Aaron a ride to practice and she mentioned it. Aaron said that he had been forwarded a site from another football player but he never watched it.

"I didn't question him again, because I didn't want to believe that he watched it and I didn't want to go there," she said.

One evening Aaron left his phone in the living room after going to bed. When his phone rang, she looked at it. She and Aaron often went through each other's phones—Aaron didn't have a lock on his—and she began scrolling through his text messages.

"It was a conversation with a male," she told me. "I started reading through it. They were talking about meeting up, and it was a little bit sexual," she said. The next day she asked him about it. He just took the phone and locked it and never brought it up again.

"There were times where I felt he almost opened up to me about what was going on with him, because he trusted me, but he didn't want to hurt me. It sucked, because I loved him."

Aaron said he wanted to get Alyssa pregnant.

"I laughed at him like he was crazy," she said. "He really wanted a family."

"One of the reasons I want to be with you," he told her, "is because you're somebody who keeps me out of trouble. I'm afraid that when I make it and when I get a lot of money, I won't know what to do," he said.

"What do you mean?" she asked.

"You don't know and see that side of me," he said. "I love drugs too much."

"Aaron," she said, "you are going to have a decision to make. Drugs are going to be there, but I am not going to be someone who keeps you off of that. You are going to have to want that."

MY COUSIN ARRANGED A graduation party for Aaron at a family member's house, but Aaron refused to invite our mother. After the party was over, he drove to our mother's house to ask her to deposit the checks he'd received as gifts.

"Are you kidding me?" my mom told Aaron. "You didn't invite me to your graduation party and you expect me to help you? No way."

Aaron kicked the side of our mother's car. She called the police and then quickly hung up. When an officer phoned back, my mother and Aaron had both cooled down and she told the officer that she was in an argument with her son but they would handle it. The police never came.

A few days later, I caught Aaron smoking marijuana with some of his old friends. “Aaron, you can’t smoke weed and be a college football player,” I told him. “You get drug tested. These guys you are with have nothing to lose.”

“I pick and choose my own friends,” Aaron said. He carried on the conversation as if there were nothing wrong with what he was doing.

CHAPTER 12

FALL 2007

GAME DAYS WERE SPECIAL.

In the morning, before we left for the stadium, I'd watch ESPN in my hotel room. I couldn't wait to hear about Florida. I'd call Aaron and he'd be in his hotel room doing the same thing. He would joke with me that UConn would never get mentioned on ESPN, and that some of his teammates didn't even know UConn had a football team.

Then late in the 2007 season, our team jumped Florida in the rankings. We were No. 16 and the Gators fell to No. 18. I pointed this out to Aaron one November morning.

"Holy cow, D, you guys are really ranked higher than us," he said. "What conference do you play in again?" We both cracked up laughing. We both knew the Southeastern Conference (SEC) schedule was tougher than ours in the Big East.

"Good luck, I love you," I'd say at the end of our conversation. He'd say it back and we'd make arrangements to speak again that night.

As a freshman, Aaron played in all thirteen games. He had 9 receptions for 151 yards and scored 2 touchdowns.

SHORTLY AFTER THE SEASON ended, Aaron called me.

"D, I want to transfer," he said.

"What's the reason, Aaron?" I asked.

"I want to go to UConn," he said.

"Aaron, you played as a freshman at *Florida*," I said. "Why would you want to transfer?"

"I just want to come home," he said.

"Why?" I asked.

"I'm not getting the ball," he said.

Shortly after our conversation he went to Coach Meyer's office and told him he wanted to transfer.

Coach Meyer explained to Aaron that his future in Gainesville was bright and that he would receive more playing time the following fall. But Aaron was adamant: he wanted out of Florida.

After several hours in Coach Meyer's office, Aaron called me.

"Coach Meyer said I was an amazing player," Aaron said. "He told me I did a great job as a freshman and that I was a great team player."

"Aaron, that's good," I said. "What did you say?"

"I said I didn't come to Florida to be a team player," Aaron said. "I told him I could be a team player anywhere in the country. I came to Florida to get the ball."

Aaron told me that several assistant coaches had also talked to him, telling him that it was in his best interest to remain in Gainesville.

Two days later, Aaron called me again. "D, I'm going to stay."

"In all honesty, I think this is the smartest decision," I said. "You guys are stacked. You *will* have a good chance to play for the national championship next season."

For a sixth time, Aaron had changed his mind. He was going to remain a Gator.

CHAPTER 13

SUMMER 2008

In the summer of 2008, I flew down south to spend time with Aaron and work out with the team. It was my first time on campus since moving my brother into his dorm eighteen months earlier. Aaron couldn't wait to introduce me to the players and his coaches, and give me a tour of the campus and the football facilities.

The first place he brought me was to the stadium: I had never seen a structure so massive. He told me to touch the grass. I laughed and bent down and felt the short-cut grass just like he had when he first visited. He was right: it felt like carpet.

For the workout, we ran gassers—we sprinted across the field and back several times—as their strength coach exhorted everyone to pick up the pace. I struggled to keep up with the speed of the Florida athletes.

Afterward, Aaron and I walked to the practice field to continue working with backup quarterback Cam Newton and cornerback Joe Hayden—both future NFL first-round draft picks.

First, Aaron and Joe raced forty yards. They tied. Then I challenged Aaron to a race. As we neared the finish line, he looked back at me with his smile. He beat me by two yards and made it look easy as I strained to keep up.

Then I caught a few passes from Cam while Joe covered me. Aaron watched from the side and then did a few reps against Joe. I had never seen such raw talent.

Once we finished, we walked outside the stadium to where Aaron and his teammates had parked their scooters.

"Okay, hold on tight," he said. "There are a lot of sand patches around and if we hit one we could go down." He said he had fallen a few times.

That was enough for me not to want to hop on.

"D, I am joking," he said. "Get on, stop being a baby. I will drive slow."

Never topping 15 miles per hour, we motored to his dorm. I was terrified, wrapping my arms around his waist.

He introduced me to his suitemate, Riley Cooper, a wide receiver on the team. We walked through their joint bathroom and back to Aaron's room. Aaron had his *Cars* bedding set—the same one my mother bought for him at Walmart the day we moved him in. He was so thrilled to have *Cars* blankets and sheets. It reminded me that Aaron, deep inside, was still a little kid.

"Soooo, there's only one bed?" I said.

He put his hand on top of his head and started rubbing his hair while looking around the room. I could tell it hadn't dawned on him to figure out sleeping arrangements.

"You could sleep here, D," he said, pointing to the floor. He then sprawled down on it. "D, it's comfortable down here," he said, smiling. "And it's nice and cool. It's hot here in Florida. Remember, heat rises so now you don't have to worry about getting hot at night."

I couldn't help but laugh.

"Oh wait," he said and then ran into the bathroom. I thought he was going to ask Riley for an air mattress, but Aaron came back with several clean white towels. "You can put these down on the floor as your mattress," he said.

He left again and then returned like he had saved the day. In his hands, he now had a bigger towel. "D, you can use this as your blanket," he said. That night, underneath the long white towel and looking at my uncovered toes below, I shivered in the air-conditioning. I didn't care. I was just happy to be with my brother again.

THE NEXT DAY AARON gave me a tour of the football facility. We chatted for a few minutes with Tim Tebow, who was watching game tape in a film room, and Aaron introduced me to his position coach, John Hevesy, who had us stand side by side because he thought we looked like twins.

We then met the graduate assistants on staff. I wanted to pursue coaching, and the GAs were generous enough to answer my questions. As we were talking, Coach Urban Meyer stepped out of his office.

Coach Meyer told us to take a seat in his office. From behind his desk, he spoke with a bluntness that caught me by surprise. "Aaron will either be the best tight end to ever play this game, or I fear he will spend the rest of his life in prison," he said. "I'm worried about the people he hangs out with outside of the program. DJ, I know you want to become a coach. After you are done playing, why don't you come down here and we'll try to find something for you so you can look after Aaron."

I told Coach Meyer that Aaron and I would talk about it, but I couldn't uproot my life and move to Florida to be a babysitter. I thanked Coach Meyer for his honesty before leaving his office.

Once we were outside, I said, "What the fuck is going on, Aaron? You need to straighten up. Are you an idiot?"

"Nothing is wrong, D," Aaron said. "You don't understand."

For the rest of my stay, Aaron became more distant. But I still tried to connect with him.

"What happened at the bar last year?" I asked. I knew our mom had to hire a lawyer for him after a fight.

"I was out with Tebow and everything was fine and someone said they would take care of the two drinks I had. As we were leaving, some guy who worked there started yelling at me and then grabbed me. He said, 'You need to pay for your drinks.' I told him someone else was paying and Tebow even offered to pay for the drinks to calm him down. And the guy said to me, 'No, you're paying for these drinks.'

"And then I walked away and the guy bumped into me. He kept brushing his chest up against me, acting like a tough guy. So I punched him in the ear. I shouldn't have done it. It was stupid."

When I left, I hoped that Aaron would straighten up.

THE WEEK BEFORE FLORIDA'S 2008 season opener, my mom told me that Aaron had failed a drug test and wouldn't be playing against Hawaii. I had thought he was sitting out because of a hamstring injury. So I called Aaron.

"Look at the opportunity you have," I said. "What are you doing?"

"It's going to be fine," Aaron said. "I'm going to be back next week. Hawaii stinks anyway."

"Aaron, enough is enough," I said. "I love you, but you have got to grow up."

"I know, D," Aaron mumbled. "I know."

I hung up the phone wondering one thing: was Aaron listening to anyone?

I THOUGHT THE SUSPENSION would scare Aaron enough so it wouldn't happen again.

For several months, Aaron quit smoking marijuana. "But he would wake up in the middle of the night having a nightmare because he thought he smoked," Alyssa said. "He would jump and then wake me up and say, 'Did I smoke? Did I?' "

The coaches at Florida started paying more attention to Aaron outside of the facility walls. During his sophomore year, Aaron essentially moved in with his position coach, John Hevesy. Hevesy wanted Aaron to experience the warmth of his loving home. Aaron grew to admire him.

Aaron appeared to be on the right path. He had a strong performance in the 2009 national title game against Oklahoma, in which Florida rolled to a 24–14 victory. A few minutes after the final whistle, Aaron ran over to our mother and me to give us a hug. I thought that Aaron's struggles were a thing of the past. For the first time in a long time, the wall he had put up against our mother had been lowered.

AARON'S FINAL COLLEGE GAME was on January 1, 2010, at the Allstate Sugar Bowl in New Orleans, where Florida defeated Cincinnati, 51–24.

I met with Coach Meyer and another assistant before the game at the team hotel near the Superdome.

"Aaron needs to go to the NFL," a Gator assistant told me, "because he may never make it out of Florida if he doesn't leave now."

The coaches were worried that Aaron would miss his entire senior season because of his excessive marijuana use and the likelihood of more failed drug tests. All I knew was one thing: if Aaron wanted to smoke, he was going to smoke. Period. End of story.

Following the bowl game, Aaron and I flew out to California, where he began training for the NFL Combine, where NFL teams evaluate draft-eligible players. But then he hurt his back during workouts.

Aaron had experienced recurring back problems at Florida. He had received seven epidurals and there were times he could barely walk. Other times his back hurt so badly he had difficulty breathing. Aaron never wanted to show that he was in pain—a lesson from our father.

The back injury he suffered in California meant he couldn't participate in any of the physical tests held at the NFL Combine in Indianapolis, where NFL prospects showcase their physical ability every February. Prior to the start of the Combine, Aaron received another epidural so he could walk normally and meet with teams.

A few weeks later, with his back pain relieved, Aaron took part in Florida's Pro Day, an event where NFL coaches and scouts came to campus to evaluate the Gators' top prospects.

Afterward, he called me.

"How did you do?" I asked.

"Good," he said. "But I didn't run the greatest."

"Mom told me you did great on the bench press, though," I said.

"Why do you think I did thirty reps of 225 pounds?" Aaron asked.

"What do you mean?"

"Because I was high," he said. "Don't tell me I can't perform when I'm smoking."

CHAPTER 14

APRIL 2010

THREE DAYS BEFORE THE NFL Draft, the arrangements had been made: our entire family was going to watch the draft at our mother's house in Connecticut.

I was in the car with Aaron on our way to meet them when our mom called me and said, "I'm done. I'm not doing it."

"What's going on?"

Aaron had told her that he wouldn't attend if Jeff was present.

I turned to Aaron and said, "Mom canceled. She doesn't want anyone to come over."

Aaron didn't say much. I told him that we could watch the draft at my apartment with his agent, my fiancée, and one of his high school friends.

"Okay, that's fine," he said.

At my apartment, I could tell Aaron was nervous. He was biting the fingernail on his right index finger nonstop. His agent pulled me aside to tell me that this could be a long few days. "There are teams that love Aaron, but there are teams that won't touch him because of their concerns about his character," he said. "There's a chance he could drop pretty far."

The first round passed and Aaron wasn't picked. "I didn't think my name would get called today," Aaron said. We all believed Aaron would be selected in the second or third round on the second day of the draft.

The next evening, the five of us were back on my living room sectional, our eyes glued to the television. More names were called from the podium in New York City. I started pacing the hardwood floor behind the couch, concerned that Aaron might not be picked at all. During commercial breaks, I'd go outside with Aaron's agent and we'd skip rocks on the gravel driveway as we discussed Aaron's draft status.

I questioned everything. Did Aaron make the right decision leaving school early? Did his past mistakes cost him a shot at being drafted? Is he even going to get drafted? What will he do if football doesn't work out for him?

The second round ended. Then the third round ended.

I told Aaron, "I hope you realize how much your decisions at Florida hurt you. You are a first-round talent."

"It's going to be okay, D," he said. "There's nothing I can do now. I just want to get drafted and prove to them what kind of player I am and prove to them that I'm going to be the best tight end ever."

"Aaron, your ability was never questioned," I said. "It was your decision-making."

On the third and final day of the draft, we reconvened. I was a nervous wreck. Midway through the fourth round, Aaron's cell phone rang. We all rose to our feet. Aaron answered and began walking around the room with the phone held to his ear. I followed closely behind.

"Thank you for the opportunity," Aaron said into the phone. "Thank you so much."

Aaron hung up. "I am going to be playing for New England," he said.

With the fifteenth pick in the fourth round—and the 113th pick overall—the Patriots selected my brother. New England was his favorite team as a child. He had a Drew Bledsoe jersey he often wore at recess. He was now living his childhood dream.

I was crying, and he was smiling like a kid who had just opened a Christmas gift he'd been asking for his entire life. We wrapped our arms around each other. "Don't ever do this to me again," I said. "Be smart. Be smart."

WE WENT TO A sports bar a mile from my apartment to celebrate with our family—minus our mother, who was still upset with Aaron. We played pool and everyone danced. As the night was coming to an end, I noticed Aaron walking outside. I asked him where he was going.

"I'm going to the casino," he said. Aaron planned to go to Mohegan Sun, thirty minutes away, with a friend who had been drinking.

"Why are you going to get in the car with someone who has been drinking? You just dropped to the fourth round because of the stupid decisions you made at Florida. Come on!"

I was angry, shouting at Aaron, telling him not to go.

Gerry, one of our older cousins, came outside and tried talking some sense into Aaron, but he wouldn't listen to him, either. Then a few of Aaron's friends approached me and said I was overreacting. I became emotional as Aaron walked toward the car. Gerry placed his left arm around me and said, "All you can do is try. If he refuses to listen to you, there is nothing you can do."

FIVE DAYS AFTER THE draft, I flew back to Europe, where I was completing my second season as a player-coach for an American football team in Klagenfurt, Austria.

Aaron and I talked face-to-face on Skype and he often repeated, "I can't believe I'm a New England Patriot!" with the enthusiasm of a little kid. But Aaron was still a kid—at age twenty, he was the youngest player in the NFL.

I also emailed Aaron articles that mentioned his past mistakes, because I wanted him to remain humble and know that he still had a lot of room for improvement.

When I returned to Connecticut after six weeks in Austria, I accepted a job as the head football coach at Southington High School in Connecticut. When Aaron had time off from training with the Patriots, he would drive two hours to train with our team. He worked with all the skilled players on their quickness and route-running techniques. Aaron's face shined when he helped a kid complete a drill that he had been struggling with.

CHAPTER 15

FALL 2010

On September 12, the sky was blue, the leaves were starting to turn orange and yellow, and the air was warm as I walked with my mother toward Gillette Stadium in Foxborough, Massachusetts, where the Patriots were hosting the Cincinnati Bengals—Aaron's first NFL regular season game. Kickoff was at 1 p.m.

We moved through the turnstile and started looking for our seats, but before we reached them I grabbed my mother by the arm. "I'm going back down to get closer to the field," I said. "I've got to see Aaron warm up."

I descended the stadium steps, marveling at all the fans in their Patriot jerseys as the pregame music blared. I imagined one day seeing hordes of fans adorned in Aaron's number with his last name on the back, cheering him on.

I neared the bottom row of the stands, directly behind one of the goalposts. At the top of my lungs I yelled, "AARON!" He didn't hear me. I tried again and started waving my hands over my head. He finally turned. He raised his right hand to his face mask and then extended it at me like he was blowing me a kiss. I thought about how emotional our dad would be if he were here.

I went back up to join my mother at our seats to watch the game, our eyes glued to Aaron whenever he was on the field.

Then it happened. With 11:27 remaining in the first quarter and the Patriots facing a first-and-ten on their own 41-yard line, Tom

Brady took the snap. He dropped back before firing a short pass to the left side of the field.

Aaron caught the ball in stride and turned on the speed. On his first NFL reception, Aaron gained 45 yards to the Bengals 14-yard line. I was screaming as loud as I could. The Patriots won the game, 38–24.

The next week against the Jets, Aaron caught six passes for 101 yards, becoming the youngest player since 1960 to top 100 receiving yards in a single game. Seven days later, against the Bills, he led the Patriots in receiving with six catches for 65 yards. He also had one rush for 13 yards.

Aaron finished the season with 45 catches for 563 yards and 6 touchdowns.

IN THE OFF-SEASON, AARON had to have hip surgery to repair a slight muscle tear. In February, shortly after his procedure, I invited Aaron and five of my friends, including our high school football coach, to my bachelor party. Aaron rented a party bus for the group to ride to Atlantic City, New Jersey, but at the last moment, Aaron told me he wouldn't go unless he brought two of his high school friends.

"Aaron, come on, you're my best man," I said. "It's for two days. You can leave your friends for two days."

He said okay and that he understood. But when the party bus arrived at my apartment, his two friends were sitting in the back. I let it go.

Still recovering from his surgery, Aaron was in a wheelchair. He paid the party bus driver to be his official wheelchair pusher for the night. We ate dinner at a Brazilian steak house. Aaron ordered chicken fingers off the kids' menu, cracking up everyone at the table. Aaron's friends laughed along, but they stayed to themselves the entire night.

After dinner, we went to a club. Aaron sat off to the side with our coach the entire time, and they shared stories about his playing days in Bristol. This was when Aaron was always his happiest—talking about the times when he was surrounded by friends and family, by love.

Our waitress had a Florida Gators logo on her cell phone screen saver.

"You're a Gators fan?" our coach asked.

"Oh my gosh, I love the Gators," she said.

"What do you think of that Hernandez guy?" he asked, with Aaron sitting next to him in his wheelchair.

"He's such a great player," she said.

"I think he sucks," our coach said. "Did you see him throw the ball into the stands against Florida State? Who does he think he is?"

"I was there! It was crazy. It was the best play of the game."

Then Aaron spoke up. "He's a bum," Aaron said. "I'm a Florida State fan." Aaron started doing the Seminole Tomahawk chop with his right hand.

"You guys don't know what you're talking about," she said as she turned and left.

We doubled over in laughter.

We called it a night and headed to our hotel. Aaron was rolled to his room. The next morning as we gathered in the lobby to leave, Aaron and his two friends were nowhere to be found. I went back to his hotel room door and knocked—no answer. I walked the casino floor. An hour after we were scheduled to leave, I finally got a key to his room from the front desk and opened the door.

Aaron was tucked under the covers of the king-size bed with his two friends, their shirts off, even though it was a luxury suite with multiple beds

"Hey, what the hell are you doing?" I asked. "We're all waiting for you so we can leave."

Aaron popped up. "Uh, we'll be right down," he said, as the other two began to stir.

Once we got home, I shut my bedroom door in my apartment so Aaron and I could have privacy, away from the other guys in my living room. I asked Aaron if he was gay.

"If you are, I don't care," I said. "I love you. You are my brother."

"Don't you ever ask me that again," Aaron said. "If you say that again, I'll fucking kill you."

CHAPTER 16

FALL 2011

ON MARCH 4, AT St. Matthew's Church in Bristol, Aaron stood next to me at the altar. The doors opened and my bride appeared. As she neared me, I felt a squeeze on my right shoulder. I looked at Aaron and he was crying—one of the few times I'd seen him shed a tear since we lost our father.

At the reception, Aaron gave the best-man speech at the Aqua Turf Club in Southington. He was full of jokes. "Hey listen, if there are any cans in here, make sure you give them to my brother," he said. "Because if we were at a party, DJ would be the one who would ask, 'Hey, are you done with that can?' My brother would collect the cans so the next day he could take them to the grocery store to collect a nickel."

Everyone laughed.

"And make sure when it's time to eat, we eat," he said. "And when it's time to dance, we dance. Because you know my brother and his damn itineraries. He's so damn particular."

More laughter ensued.

EIGHT MONTHS LATER, ON November 6, 2011, the Patriots hosted the New York Giants at Gillette Stadium. Aaron caught 4 passes for 35 yards and a touchdown, but New England lost, 24–20.

I watched the game from my office in Providence, Rhode Island, where I was working as the quarterbacks coach at Brown University.

On Sundays, the staff began formulating our game plan for the upcoming opponent, and we usually didn't leave until after midnight, which meant I would miss Aaron's twenty-second birthday party that night.

My mom drove from Bristol to Aaron's condo, which was only a few miles from Gillette Stadium. She was hoping that this would be a night to celebrate Aaron and all that he had accomplished. All she wanted was an enjoyable, fight-free evening with her son.

She walked in and saw a buffet of food spread out on the kitchen table. Aaron's girlfriend, Shayanna, whom he had reconnected with since returning from Florida, had put together a tower of cupcakes. Some of his friends made my mom nervous. One friend, who went by the name Sherrod, aka Alexander Bradley, was a convicted drug dealer from East Hartford, Connecticut. He was one of many bad influences now hovering in Aaron's inner circle.

My mother went downstairs to have a cigarette. She opened the door to the garage and there was Aaron, alone in the dark, sitting on the hood of his black Range Rover, cleaning a handgun.

"Aaron, what are you doing?" our mom asked, concerned. "Why do you have a gun? Are you stupid?"

Aaron lifted his eyes and flashed a disgusted look. He remained silent and kept cleaning his gun. My mom went back inside.

A few minutes later Aaron was called upstairs for the celebration. As soon as he appeared in front of his cake, his smile was back—the fun-loving, approachable Aaron had returned. My mother was stunned at his transformation. Moments earlier he seemed withdrawn and depressed and in a bad mental place; now he was a picture of happiness.

Everyone sang "Happy Birthday" before Aaron blew out his candles. He asked one of his friends to arrange for a party bus to come to his place. The destination: a Boston nightclub. Our mom would not be joining them.

"AARON WASN'T THE KID I remembered," our mom told me later. "It was like he wasn't my kid anymore. His attitude was getting worse and worse. I had no clue what was going on with him and couldn't understand his selection of friends. I knew he was going the wrong way and I told him this. But he was drifting further and further away. He would call me and say, 'I hate you because you don't even know me.' That really hurt."

THE PARTY BUS ARRIVED. One of our cousins and her boyfriend hadn't planned on going out, and they weren't dressed appropriately for a night on the town, so they told Aaron they couldn't go.

"You're about the same size as Shayanna, so you could wear some of her clothes," Aaron said. "And your boyfriend can wear something of mine."

Once everyone was dressed, they filed onto the party bus. On board, my cousin offered to chip in for the expenses. Then Sherrod stood up and said, "Nah, I got it. Right, Aaron? You don't ever have to touch your pockets when you with me, Aaron, right? Tell 'em."

Sherrod made my cousin feel uncomfortable. "Sherrod kept talking about how much everything cost," she told me. "He would be like, 'Do you see these bracelets right here? This is worth ten thousand dollars.' He went on and on, saying this diamond is worth this, and this is worth that. I remember sitting there with everyone and thinking, *Who is this clown and why is he here?*"

THAT WAS A QUESTION all of us asked when we met Sherrod. The first time I was introduced to him, I had arrived at Aaron's condo after watching him play at Gillette Stadium. I walked inside and sat in the living room with a few family members. We were talking when I spotted a man I didn't recognize walking up the stairs from the ground-floor entrance. I was looking in his direction because I thought it was Aaron coming back from his game. But it was Sherrod.

He was about six feet tall, light-skinned, wearing glasses, and had short hair in waves. Without saying a word or making any eye contact, he walked through our conversation and continued on past the kitchen, down the hall, and up the stairs, where no one was at the time.

As he strutted past us, my aunt saw the look on my face—a look that said, "Who the hell is this?" My aunt caught my attention and mouthed the word "Trouble" while shaking her head very slowly.

A few minutes later, I heard the door shut downstairs and then footsteps. It was Aaron. He came up behind me, gave me a hug, and smiled at everyone in the room. We started talking about the game until Sherrod came back down the stairs.

It was like a balloon popped, the way Aaron's demeanor changed. He became visibly uneasy.

THE PARTY BUS PULLED up to the Cure Lounge. Several of Aaron's Patriot teammates were inside. Aaron and his guests sat at tables near them.

At one point Aaron stepped out of the club into a private area to smoke a joint. Our cousin asked him, "Are you sure that's okay? You're not going to smell? Aren't people watching you, Aaron?"

Aaron smiled back at her. "It's all good," he said. "They let me do it here all the time."

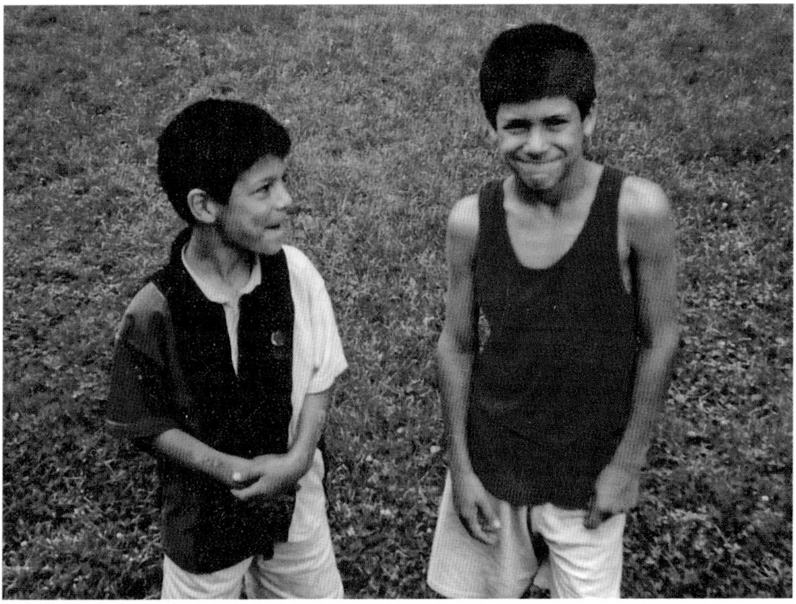

Aaron (*left*) and me playing in our grandparents' backyard.

Christmas Eve in our living room.

(All photographs are courtesy of the Hernandez family unless otherwise noted.)

Playing with our dad and our German shepherd, UConn, in our driveway.

A family photo with our mother and father after Aaron's eighth-grade graduation. He's wearing our father's favorite tie.

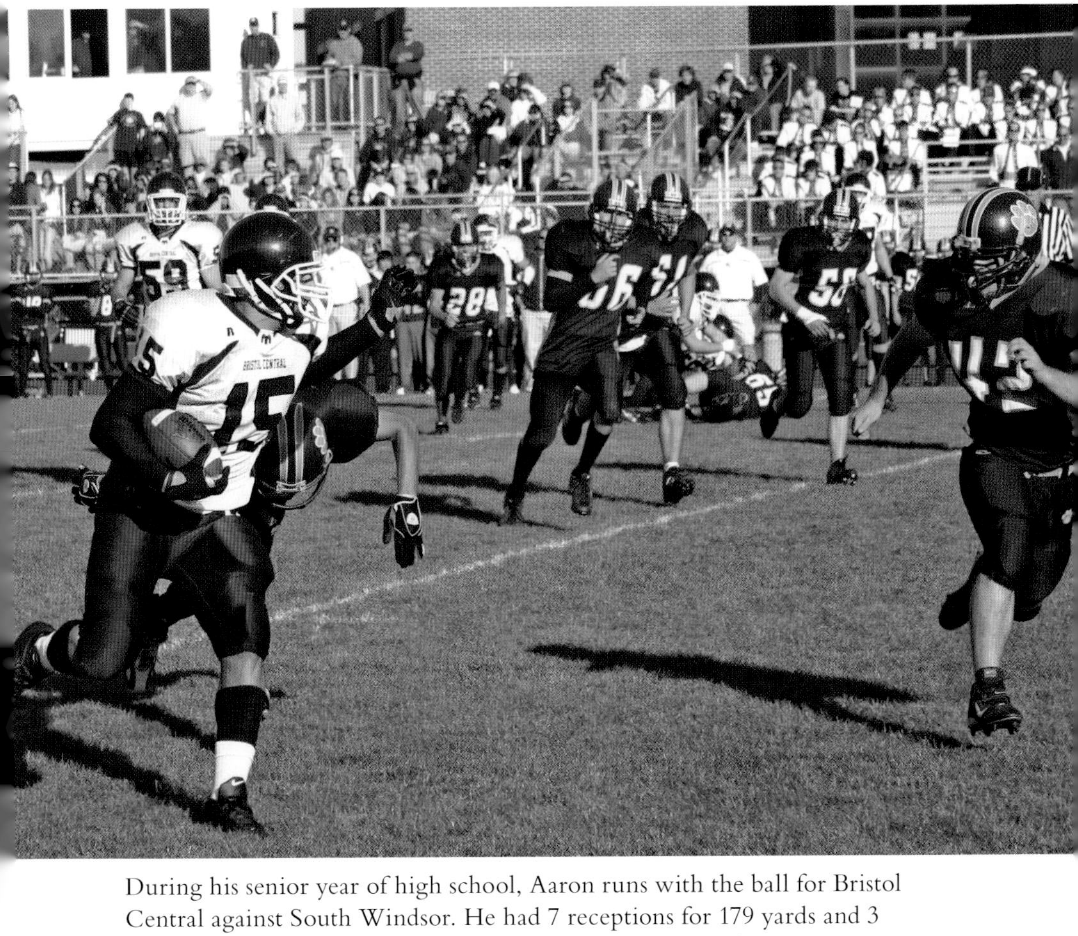

During his senior year of high school, Aaron runs with the ball for Bristol Central against South Windsor. He had 7 receptions for 179 yards and 3 touchdowns in the first half. (*David Greenleaf/Bristol Central*)

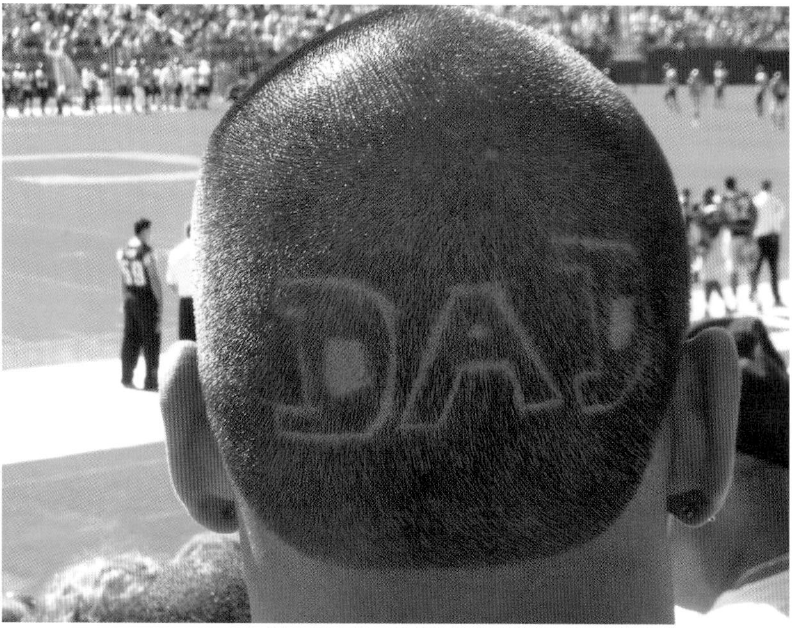

In memory of our father, Aaron had "DAD" shaved into the back of his head.

Aaron signing papers to declare for the NFL draft.

With Aaron in Los Angeles in January 2010.

Aaron and our mother at the Walter Camp National Awards banquet in New Haven, Connecticut, following his final season at Florida.

With Aaron on my wedding day, March 4, 2011, as the bride walked down the aisle. (*Jennifer Fiereck/J. Fiereck Photography*)

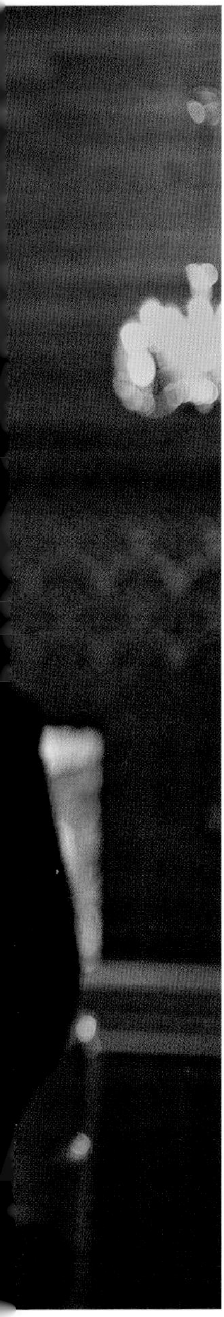

Embracing Aaron the night he was drafted by the Patriots, April 24, 2010.

With our cousins at a family Christmas party, December 24, 2012.

Together on the field at Lucas Oil Stadium, in Indianapolis, before Super Bowl XLVI.

Wes Welker (*right*) watches Aaron's "Make It Rain" touchdown celebration after scoring in the third quarter of Super Bowl XLVI.
(Rob Carr/Super Bowl XLVI/Getty Images)

CHAPTER 17

JANUARY 14, 2012

The evening began with so much promise, so much joy at Gillette Stadium.

The temperature had dipped into the teens—my breath shot out in white puffs—but man, I was so proud as I watched my younger brother during pregame warm-ups for the divisional playoff game against the Denver Broncos.

On this winter evening in New England, Aaron was as dominating as ever, as versatile as ever. He lined up all over the field: tight end, wide receiver, and running back. Aaron caught 4 passes for 55 yards and 1 touchdown while rushing for 61 yards. It was hard to fathom that a player with that much talent was related to me. New England won the game, 45–10.

After the game, Aaron was asked in the locker room by reporters if he would be ready for the AFC Championship Game the following Sunday. "I feel great," Aaron said. "I love running back. I hope [Coach Bill Belichick] keeps letting me do it. Doesn't matter, whatever I can do to help this team to get to the next game."

Once Aaron was finished with his team responsibilities, I met him outside the locker room—unaware that the medical staff had examined him for a head injury in the fourth quarter. A Patriots employee then guided Aaron, my wife, two of his friends, and myself onto a golf cart and drove us to Aaron's SUV, parked in a private lot for the players.

Aaron was quiet but seemed content, satisfied, ready to head home and enjoy a relaxing evening at his condominium. Aaron got in the driver's side. Aaron usually let others do the driving, but tonight he felt like being in control of the vehicle. I took a seat in back.

Aaron flipped on the ignition and pulled out of the lot at a slow roll. We approached a police officer directing traffic. Aaron inched closer until the officer extended his hand, signaling for us to stop.

The wheels at rest, the engine idling, I noticed Aaron's eyes moving back and forth from the officer to somewhere to his right. He looked like he was panicking. Then, without saying anything, Aaron slammed down on the gas pedal, nearly striking the cop in front of us and the oncoming traffic.

I turned my head back at the officer Aaron had almost hit. "What the *fuck* are you doing?" I yelled to Aaron from the backseat as I watched the officer rush to his cruiser. "Pull over. He's coming. His lights are on."

The officer was twenty-five yards behind us. Aaron hit the accelerator harder, causing my head to snap back, the engine now in full thunder. Suddenly we were speeding down a dark and narrow back road with a police cruiser chasing us. Aaron jumped from lane to lane to race around the cars in front of us, while also dodging oncoming headlights.

"Stop the car, Aaron, please stop the car!"

Aaron ignored my words; it was as if he were alone in the vehicle. I again looked back at the oncoming officer, who was now only a few cars behind us, the red-and-blue lights flashing in the dark night. One of Aaron's friends thought it was funny and was laughing.

"What the fuck are you doing? Pull over," I pleaded. "Why are you running from the cops? Aaron, you're going to kill us!"

I jabbed Aaron on his right shoulder—he didn't say one word.

After a few minutes, Aaron took a hard right—my body was thrown to the left as Aaron snapped the wheel down. I squeezed the front passenger's headrest with my hands, bracing myself, fearful that the SUV would tip and roll.

He slammed on the brakes—I could feel the SUV slide until it came to a standstill, just to the left of a dark storage unit. Aaron turned off his car and stared in the rearview mirror.

"What are you thinking, Aaron?" I yelled.

"Calm down," he said, as the cop zipped by and disappeared into the distance.

He turned the SUV's low beams back on, grabbed the steering wheel, backed up over the gravel, and then drove off. He never said another word about it.

From the backseat, I was consumed with one question: *What is going on with my brother?*

CHAPTER 18

FEBRUARY 5, 2012

ARRIVING AT OUR SEATS, I couldn't sit down. I had butterflies in my stomach: my brother was playing in the Super Bowl! Kelly Clarkson was introduced to sing the national anthem. The drums rattled and the crowd quieted. Her powerful voice echoed. Aaron and I had watched her compete on season one of *American Idol*; now my brother stood fifty feet from her.

Looking up at the Jumbotron, I saw Tom Brady, his eye-black neatly swiped, mouthing the words of the anthem. I scanned the crowd, looking at all the cameras flashing. Then I lifted my gaze back up at the Jumbotron. There was my brother on the big screen, slowly swaying back and forth, like he had before his thousand-point game in high school.

I thought about all the times Aaron and I watched the Super Bowl in our living room, on our version of a big screen. Before the game we would watch our dad prepare his own special recipe of chicken wings, Frank's hot sauce, a stick of butter, and several shakes of garlic salt. Then we would unfold our four wooden trays in front of our spots on the sofa. Nibbling on the wings, as a family, we would embrace the Super Bowl action together.

THE PATRIOTS LED 10–9 at halftime. Early in the third quarter, facing a second and two at the Giants twelve-yard line, New England lined up with no running backs in the backfield—an "empty" formation. From my seat, I could see that Aaron would be isolated against a linebacker in the middle of the field. Aaron loved one-on-one matchups because it gave him the ability to use his quickness and athleticism in the open field. My eyes were glued to him as the ball was snapped.

Aaron fired out of his stance to press the defender back on his heels. Aaron stopped on a dime, then gave the linebacker a hard juke and head fake to the outside before cutting underneath him to the inside. Brady delivered a quick strike to Aaron, who turned up the field and crossed the goal line for a touchdown. The Patriots led 17–9.

But New England couldn't put the Giants away. With less than a minute remaining in the game, New England trailed 21–17 and had the ball on its twenty-yard line. On first-and-ten, Brady and Deion Branch couldn't connect over the middle. On second-and-ten, Aaron dropped a pass across the middle from Brady.

Then Brady was sacked, forcing New England to take their final time-out with 36 second left. On fourth-and-16, Brady eluded the rush, flipped his hips, and fired a pass down the left sideline to Branch for a 19-yard gain before stepping out of bounds, stopping the clock with 32 seconds.

The next play, Aaron caught another ball from Brady, this one an 11-yard gain to the Patriots 44-yard line. Nineteen seconds remained.

Two plays later, with five seconds left, New England had the ball on its own 49-yard line. There was time for one last play.

"Please, Father, help us," I prayed.

The ball was snapped. Brady shuffled around in the pocket, avoiding the three-man rush, and then heaved it as high and as far as he could. I looked to the end zone: Aaron was preparing to catch the Hail Mary.

Aaron set his feet to jump in the middle of the end zone as five defenders collapsed around him. Aaron leapt and extended his arms, but one of the New York defensive backs hit the ball just before it touched Aaron's fingertips. End over end, the ball fell to the turf. The game was over. New York won 21–17.

Aaron, who had caught a team-high eight passes for 67 yards and one touchdown, dropped to the ground. I watched him closely; it was as if the loss had caused his body to fall limp. He sat in the end zone in shock. His teammate Rob Gronkowski helped him to his feet. It was more than a game.

Later that night I stood in a long line outside an Indianapolis hotel with other team family members waiting to attend a postgame celebration. I was with my wife and mother.

"Hey, where did you sit?" I asked my mom. I had tried to find her in the stands before the game started but I couldn't see her.

"I was so embarrassed," my mother said. "I sat down and here comes Aaron's friend Bo with a prostitute. And they sat right next to us. It was ridiculous. Why would Aaron invite them and why would he sit them right next to me?"

I was taken aback by this news. Minutes later, I spotted Aaron exiting a vehicle with Tanya and his friend Sherrod. Aaron and Sherrod wore matching outfits: blue Gucci shirts with little *G*'s scattered in a pattern, the same pants and similar shoes.

I caught up to Aaron and told him that we had a spot saved in line. He said to follow him. I ran back and told my wife and mother that Aaron said to come with him.

A few hours later I saw Barry Sanders, the former Detroit Lions running back who had been my favorite player growing up. Starstruck, I put my Bud Light bottle down at the nearest table and asked him for a picture. "Please, Barry, you're my favorite player and you're one of my brother's as well," I said.

"Who is your brother?" he asked.

I told him.

"He's a good player," Barry said. "Go get him and we'll get a picture of the three of us."

I ran to grab Aaron. I told him that we could take a picture with Barry Sanders. We bolted to his side. We thanked Barry at least five times. Walking away, we stared in wonderment at the picture on my phone like the adoring kids we still were inside.

Aaron never acknowledged our mother or spoke to her that night, so she left early. "I had to leave," she said. "I was so upset and angry, I was burning up inside over how he treated me."

CHAPTER 19

SPRING 2012

AFTER THE SUPER BOWL, I resumed my life in Providence as the quarterbacks coach at Brown University. My entire identity was wrapped around football. The game kidnapped my mind and my heart. Everything else was secondary. My wife would talk to me and it was as if she were conversing with a wall. "Are you still thinking about football?" she'd ask. I would hang my head and say, "Yes." At the time, I didn't realize how mixed-up my priorities were.

My wife and I had been together for seven years and married for one. She had been with me as I weathered the storm of my father's death and helped me overcome my mother's betrayal with Jeff. She was the family I needed when my own family was falling apart.

On the weekend of our one-year anniversary my wife and I decided to celebrate in New York City together. I had to work on Friday night, and that evening she told me she planned to stay at a friend's house.

The next morning we drove two hours to Manhattan, to a hotel in the Theater District. I asked about her evening, but she didn't share many details, other than to say it had been a "low-key" night. Then, twenty minutes into our drive, she was out cold, in a deep sleep, her head resting against the passenger's window.

As I continued to drive I sensed something was wrong. I didn't understand why she was so tired.

When we reached our hotel, I pretended that everything was fine.

That night we went to the musical *Wicked* at the Gershwin Theatre—my first Broadway show. We had a great time, but I couldn't shake this lingering feeling that something wasn't right. I remember thinking, *It's probably just me and I'm overthinking the situation.*

On Sunday night we returned to our apartment in Providence. On Monday morning I gave her a kiss before heading to work. When I reached the office, I couldn't concentrate. I started to think, *Is she seeing someone else?*

I needed to figure this out. I logged on to our shared AT&T account and scanned our call history. One number stood out because it had been dialed more often than others—and at odd hours.

I pulled out a piece of paper and wrote the number down. At first I pushed in a few digits, but then talked myself out of calling, even getting mad at myself for not trusting my wife. But then I did it: I entered the numbers into my cell phone. The knot in my stomach turned tighter as the phone rang. I prayed that a woman would answer.

"Hello?" a male voice said. I hung up, and immediately found myself struggling to breathe.

Despite the evidence, I didn't want to accuse her of anything without gathering more information. Every night I would go home and try to build up the courage to ask her about the number, but I couldn't because I feared the truth.

For a few weeks, I tracked her calls. Then one evening, while she was in the bathroom preparing for another evening out, her cell phone vibrated on her nightstand. The message from an unidentified number—the same one I had noted in our call history—read: "Am I going to see you tonight?"

With her iPhone in my hand, I paced around our bedroom. I started taking deep breaths—so deep that I grew light-headed and had to sit on the edge of our bed.

I couldn't hold it in any longer. I finally went into the bathroom to confront her. She was in the shower. I slid the curtain open and held up the text message she had received. After wiping the water from her face, she looked at the phone. Her chin dropped and her eyes turned toward mine.

I was shaking as I asked, "Who is this?"

"I don't know," she said.

I asked again.

She then claimed it was a friend.

"Why don't you have this friend's number saved in your contacts like the rest of your friends?"

She looked at me for several seconds—and said nothing.

At that moment I knew my marriage was in trouble.

Several days later I called my brother. "I think my wife is seeing someone else," I said.

There was a long, silent pause on the phone. Then, "Damnnnnn. Are you okay, D? Where are you?"

"I am driving back to my house right now," I said. "I don't know what to do or where to go."

"Come over to my place," he said.

I packed a few belongings and drove to Aaron's, thirty minutes away.

Aaron greeted me at the front door. He was alone that night. We walked inside and he showed me to the second-floor bedroom. I hung up my clothes and then went to his family room, where Aaron was watching television.

Aaron kept telling me, "D, you're young. You will get through this."

But I couldn't stop thinking about the lack of love and attention I gave her. I couldn't stop beating myself up for choosing football over my wife.

I walked down the stairs and into the kitchen to boil a pot of water for macaroni and cheese. Aaron went to his bedroom. Once my food was ready, I went to see what he was doing. Entering the room, I saw the bottom drawer of his dresser open and stuffed with bags of marijuana. I grew nervous. He started introducing the bags by name as if they were people with personalities. I couldn't believe it.

After shutting the dresser drawers, Aaron peeked out his blinds and looked at the surrounding windows of other condos. I thought he was about to get busted for having so much weed.

"If I ever get caught around this shit, I'll be done," I said. "I'll be fired from Brown and there's no way in hell I'll be able to get another job."

From the other side of the room, I spotted a big kitchen knife in the top drawer of his nightstand. It was to the left of his bed, close to the window he was looking out of.

"Aaron, why the hell is that big knife in your nightstand?" I asked.

"I sleep with it because people are after me," he said. "I've got it for protection."

"Who is after you, Aaron?" I asked.

"Everyone," he said. "The FBI, everyone."

"What did you do?" I asked.

"Nothing," he said. "Nothing at all."

I was very confused by his paranoia: he genuinely believed someone was out to get him and he couldn't communicate why. At one point, he went back to the window and said, "They are probably watching us right now." I assumed he was acting this way because of the marijuana.

We walked back outside. I had to get a few more belongings out of my car and he had to throw his trash in the dumpster. We continued to talk, but in the middle of our conversation, he shifted his eyes to the left, to look at the neighbor's windows he had been staring at before from his bedroom. But he wouldn't lift his head up to look;

he only moved his eyes. He whispered, "They are watching us and listening to us right now."

Aaron's actions were starting to make *me* paranoid, enough that I told him I was going to head back home.

"D, don't worry," he said in his normal voice. "Everything's fine."

I looked at him closely. I couldn't figure him out. I decided to stay. I walked back up the stairs and went to bed.

After work the next day, I drove to Aaron's, packed my car, and told him I was going to sleep at home. He asked me to stay with him another night, but I said I couldn't.

"Is this because of last night?" he asked.

"Yes," I said.

"Everything is fine," he replied, and started laughing at me. He didn't realize how scattered his thoughts were as he worried about the people who were after him.

I didn't know what was going on, I didn't know what to do, but I knew I had to leave.

I returned home and went directly into the spare bedroom.

CHAPTER 20

SPRING 2012

A few weeks later, as my wife and I were going through divorce proceedings, I was walking across Brown's campus when my cell phone started to vibrate in my pocket. It was one of my former UConn teammates who was now a graduate assistant at the University of Miami. "The Miami coaches would like to meet with you," he told me. "There's an opening as an offensive graduate assistant on the staff. Would you be interested in flying down here for an interview?"

"Yes," I replied.

After hanging up the phone, I immediately went into the office of my head coach to make him aware of the job opportunity at Miami.

Then I phoned Aaron, asking for his advice about interviewing with the Hurricanes.

"Follow your heart, D," he said. "Plus, Miami is beautiful. You have to go look at it. Miami is big-time."

Next, I called Coach Edsall at UConn. He thought I should stay at Brown. "There are too many guys jumping around from job to job," he said. "If you do a good job at Brown, everything will work out."

I phoned other coaches for their advice and got even more conflicting opinions.

I dialed Aaron again. "Some coaches are telling me to leave Brown if I'm offered the position and some are telling me to stay," I said. "I don't know what to do."

"D," he said, laughing, "this is exactly how I felt when I was in high school trying to decide between UConn and Florida. I had so many people telling to me to stay at UConn and so many others saying it would be best for my career to go to Florida. It's crazy how things work out. But if you accept the job, I have a place you can stay in. It's right on the beach and it's a penthouse. You could stay there for a few months until you find a place of your own."

I decided to interview for the position, and I was offered the job. I went back to my head coach's office, my wedding ring no longer on my finger, and told him I was heading to Miami. He was concerned that I was running away from my failed marriage.

Days later, as I packed my belongings into the back of a U-Haul for the twenty-eight-hour drive south, Aaron stopped by my apartment.

"You're going to coach at the U! *At the U!*" he said. "You are going to do it, D. You're going to be a big-time coach one day."

I ARRIVED AT MY brother's off-season rental in Hallandale, Florida. Easing into the parking lot in my Jetta, I spotted BMWs, Bentleys, Range Rovers, and Rolls-Royces. Then I looked up: the building stretched so high that it seemed like it was puncturing the clouds. There were fifty-one floors in the oceanfront property, and Aaron's place was on the forty-eighth.

As I walked into the lobby, I must have looked like a wide-eyed tourist, the way I gazed in wonder at everything. I rode the elevator to the forty-eighth floor, opened the door to the suite, and was overwhelmed: the furniture looked like it was too expensive to even touch. Floor-to-ceiling glass windows wrapped around the entire suite. A balcony opened up to a breathtaking view of Fort Lauderdale. The back end of the suite offered a stunning view of the Atlantic Ocean.

I called Aaron, who was still in New England preparing for training camp, which was two months away. "This is the most amazing place I have ever seen," I said.

He was happy that I liked it but had a few requests: I could only sleep in the spare bedroom, I wasn't allowed to drive his Range Rover, and I had to be careful about who I let inside the place. I told him I understood; all of that sounded reasonable.

AARON AND SHAY, WHO was pregnant, showed up at the high-rise a few weeks later. The three of us spent time together talking, telling stories, and laughing. I could tell Aaron was in love. Sitting on the couch, he would gaze adoringly at her and rub and kiss her growing belly.

After a few days, they returned to New England. About a week later, I was getting ready to go out with a few other Miami coaches when I heard the front door open. I peeked my head around the corner.

It was Sherrod. He was carrying a black duffel bag over his right shoulder. He was alone.

"What's up, D?" he said as he walked past the bathroom door and into the living room. I heard a noise that sounded like something had fallen onto the ground. I left the bathroom to see what was going on.

The black duffel bag was on the kitchen floor, empty. On a glass table was a two-foot mountain of cash, all in stacks of hundred-dollar bills.

Then I saw a gun on the table—the first gun I'd ever seen outside the movies. It was silver and black and it looked very small. My heart started racing.

I tried to play it cool, because I didn't want to look weak. But inside I was terrified and thinking, *What the fuck? What the fuck? What the fuck?*

Sherrod went out onto the balcony. The doors were left open and the big white drapes were blowing inside the suite. He was pacing back and forth.

I grabbed my wallet and headed toward the front door. But then the front door opened again: it was Aaron.

"Where are you going?" Aaron asked. "You look fly."

"I'm going to meet up with some of the other coaches," I said. "I wish I knew you were coming. Why didn't you even call to let me know?"

Then I nodded my head in the direction of where the gun and the money were. "What the hell is that?"

"Don't worry about it, D," he said.

He bent down and flipped my pants up, cuffing them. "Now you look fresh," he said.

Sherrod walked back inside from the balcony and said, "D, come over here." He handed me three hundred-dollar bills. "Have fun tonight," he said.

After dinner and drinks with my fellow coaches, I returned to Aaron's apartment. All the lights were on. Aaron was alone on the sofa. The gun and the cash were no longer on the table. I sat next to him. He was holding a white iPad and staring at the screen. I inched closer to him: He was viewing Patriots practice film.

I rose to go to bed.

Aaron said, "D, I'm going to be the best tight end to ever play the game."

Seven hours later, I opened my bedroom door and Aaron was on the couch and still watching film.

"Did you sleep?" I asked.

"No. I told you I'm going to be the best tight end to ever play this game."

The next day Aaron left to return to Massachusetts. The start of training camp was approaching.

CHAPTER 21

JUNE 2012

A FEW WEEKS LATER, IN June 2012, the coaching staff at Miami had a summer break, so I went home to Bristol and stayed at a friend's house for two weeks. Jeff was living at my mother's and I didn't want to be there.

One night Aaron called and asked me if I could pick him up at Logan International Airport in Boston.

I told him I had plans with our cousin Jay; Aaron said to bring him along. Aaron also asked me to swing by his condo to grab some clothes for him on the way to the airport. He said he had rented hotel rooms in Boston and we could go out together after we picked him up.

Once Aaron got into the car, the three of us went to the hotel. Aaron took his time getting ready—he didn't like to go out until it was late, around 11:30 p.m.

There was an unexpected knock on the hotel room door. Sherrod walked in. Jay, who brought his hair clippers, was giving Aaron a haircut.

"Why do you hang out with Sherrod?" Jay asked as he was cutting Aaron's hair. "That dude isn't your real friend. He doesn't care about you."

Sherrod overheard Jay and started arguing with him. "I don't ask him for money," Sherrod said. "I don't need his money."

"What the hell does money have to do with anything?" Jay asked.

I was sitting on a chair in the corner of the red-carpeted room, drinking a Bacardi Razz and Sprite in one of the glass cups the hotel provided. All I wanted was for everyone to hurry up so we could leave.

As soon as our cousin finished trimming Aaron's hair, I said, "We didn't drive all the way up to Boston to hang out with a bunch of dudes in a hotel room all night. We're going to head out now, so just text me when you and Sherrod are ready."

Later that night we met Aaron and Sherrod at a bar near the hotel. I spotted a few basketball players I went to college with. We chatted for a few minutes about football and their playing careers in Europe. Then I went back to the bar where Aaron and Sherrod were standing.

Aaron looked like he was in a state of panic. "You trust too many people. You shouldn't be talking to those guys," he said. As he spoke, he kept looking back at them, like he thought one of my friends was planning to hit him over the head with a bottle or something.

"Aaron, I know these guys from college," I said. "We're friends."

For several minutes, Aaron didn't take his eyes off them. He was being paranoid and I didn't understand why.

The next morning Jay and I went to say good-bye to my brother. When we opened his hotel room door, we started laughing. Aaron was lying facedown under the covers with his arms and legs sprawled out and falling off both sides of the bed.

I started poking him. He didn't budge. I tried rolling him over, but he was too heavy. For a second we thought something was wrong.

I ran to the bathroom, filled up a little trash can with water, and splashed it on the back of Aaron's head.

He quickly popped up. "What the hell is going on?" he groggily said. "I'm trying to sleep."

"We got nervous because you weren't moving," Jay said.

"All I need is a blunt and I'll be all right," Aaron said.

CHAPTER 22

FALL 2012

ON FRIDAY, AUGUST 31, I was back in Massachusetts for Miami's season opener against Boston College. On the eve of the game I met one of my former teammates at a pub. Drinking a few beers and eating chicken wings, we reminisced about our playing days at UConn and overseas.

During our conversation, my iPhone chimed. The message from Aaron read: "We made it, D. We made it."

I stepped outside and called Aaron.

"We are set for life, D," he said. "I just signed a new contract worth forty million dollars and a twelve-and-a-half-million-dollar signing bonus."

I almost lost my breath. I couldn't believe it—Aaron had just received the largest signing bonus ever given to an NFL tight end. The $40 million total was the second largest extension ever for a tight end, behind his teammate Rob Gronkowski. If Aaron handled his money wisely, he would be financially stable for the rest of his life.

"The first thing I'm going to do is donate fifty thousand dollars to the Kraft family," he said. Robert Kraft, the Patriots owner, had taken a chance on Aaron in the draft two years earlier. His wife, Myra, had passed away from cancer a year earlier, and Aaron wanted to give to their foundation.

"This is just the beginning for you," I told him. "Remember that the NFL is a business and they gave you this contract for a reason. You have to keep producing."

After hanging up, I rejoined my college teammate.

"Is everything okay?" he asked.

"My brother just signed a contract extension with the Patriots," I said. Then, my phone still in my hand, it chimed again. I was amazed: Aaron had sent me an image of the $2 million deposit he had just made into his bank account. I carefully counted all the zeros and then shared the photo with my friend.

Everything in my brother's career seemed to be falling into place. He was about to start his third NFL season and he had already earned his second contract—a five-year extension. The average NFL career is about 3.3 years, and Aaron appeared to be on his way to playing much longer.

The next day we beat Boston College, 41–32.

A FEW WEEKS LATER, Aaron called me again with more big news: he was going to propose to Shayanna.

I asked Aaron if he was sure about his decision. "I don't want you to get hurt like I did," I said. "There's so much unexpected pain that can come with it."

"D, I have thought about this for a while," Aaron said. "She treats me amazing and she is going to have our princess. I love her."

Aaron had already picked out an engagement ring. Two weeks before Shayanna's baby shower—she was in her third trimester—he rented a limousine and arranged for it to pick up our mother, her sister, and our grandmother. The limo then carried them to Massachusetts to get Aaron, and the four of them went to a mall so he could show them the ring he was going to purchase.

At the mall, Aaron led the three women to a jewelry store, where he bought a diamond heart necklace for our grandmother, who cried as Aaron clasped it around her neck.

Aaron showed everyone the ring he wanted to buy Shayanna. My mother told him it had the biggest diamond she had ever seen; she wondered if Shay's finger would be able to hold it up. Aaron bought the ring.

"Aaron made all of us feel good," my mother said later. "He was so fun and loving. He was the nice Aaron. He was my baby again."

THE BABY SHOWER WAS in October at the Carousel Museum in Bristol. Midway through the shower, as Shay sat in a chair in the middle of the room, Aaron quietly entered, sucking on a lollipop. He got down on one knee and asked Shay to marry him. In tears, she said yes.

A month later, on November 6, Aaron's birthday, Avielle Janelle Hernandez was born. Aaron was excused from practice to be at Shay's side in the hospital.

He called me to share the news. "She is so precious, D," he said. *"I can't believe I'm a dad now!"*

On December 22, I returned to Boston from Florida to meet Aaron's daughter for the first time and get a tour of his new home in North Attleborough, Massachusetts. When I walked through the door, Aaron was holding baby Avielle. She was perfect, the most gorgeous human I had ever laid my eyes on. Aaron made me scrub my hands with sanitizer twice before I held her, and she immediately melted my heart. She had done the same thing to Aaron, who couldn't stop looking at her. It was a struggle just to get him to let me hold her, because he didn't want to let her out of his arms. He was fully consumed by his baby.

He showed me around his beautiful home, which featured five bedrooms, six bathrooms, a hot tub, a sauna, a theater room, a backyard pool, and a massive playhouse. I couldn't stop thinking about how his garage was bigger than our childhood home.

The next day the Patriots hosted Jacksonville. Aaron had one catch for 13 yards in New England's 23–16 win.

The following evening we had our annual Christmas gathering at a cousin's house in Bristol. Aaron showed up without the baby.

"I didn't want to bring Avielle because I don't want her to get sick, so she is home with Shay," he said. For several minutes, as Aaron and I talked, he appeared happy and so content. The brother I knew was by my side.

Then, as suddenly as a lit candle blows out, Aaron changed. He quit talking. He quit smiling. He seemed preoccupied, focusing on something only he knew about.

I asked a family member to take a picture of Aaron, me, and two of our cousins. When I looked at the photo, I noticed that everyone was smiling except Aaron. "Aw, Aaron, you didn't smile," I said. "Let's take another one."

We retook the picture. The result was the same: Aaron still had a dark expression on his face.

"Aaron, what's wrong?" I asked. "Why aren't you smiling?"

"I was," he said.

We took another photo—same result. I finally gave up.

CHAPTER 23

JANUARY 2013

After the holidays, I returned to Florida. I carried my luggage into the apartment I had finally rented in Miami and dove onto my brown sofa to relax after my flight. The scent of trash filled the apartment from the dumpster outside my broken sliding-glass door. I was still struggling with being alone after my divorce.

The next day my fortunes changed: I was offered a job at the University of Iowa as a graduate assistant. At Iowa, I would be responsible for coaching the tight ends—I missed being a position coach.

I told the Miami head coach how much I appreciated working on his staff before I accepted the position, and I booked a flight to Iowa.

I spent the first two nights in Iowa City sleeping on a couch in the football facility. On the second night I was awakened by a custodian vacuuming the players lounge. He must have told offensive line coach Brian Ferentz—the son of head coach Kirk Ferentz—that he found me there because the next morning Brian poked his head into my office and invited me to stay in a spare bedroom in his house until I found my own apartment.

That night, Brian, who had coached my brother in New England, invited me out for a pizza dinner. Once we ordered, he started talking football. He cleared space on the table and, using salt and pepper shakers and sugar packets, began moving them around as if they were players on a football field. He pulled a pen out of his pocket and began teaching me zone-blocking schemes. Immediately I was sold.

My father had briefly played with Coach Kirk Ferentz at UConn. Whenever we had watched Iowa play in our living room, he raved about him, saying what a great man he was—a man of character and kindness. When I received a recruiting letter from Iowa in high school, my father proudly posted it on the refrigerator. They never offered me a scholarship—I knew I wasn't a national prospect—but my father continued to tell me how special the coach who led the Hawkeye program was.

On my third day, I went to Brian's office and we started studying Patriots practice film of my brother and Rob Gronkowski. I took notes, writing down every word he was saying. He told me to put my pen down and just watch the tape with him. He said I could look at his own notebooks—the first time a coach had ever been willing to share his own football secrets with me.

I found an apartment and my outlook on life turned sunny. The people I was around each day cared for me and looked out for me. The Iowa program was one big family.

I called Aaron often and told him about the coaches and how family-oriented everyone was.

"D, I love how happy you sound," Aaron said. "Your time is coming. You are with the best, and I know one day you are going to be a big-time D1 coach. I can feel it, D. Just keep working hard."

IN FEBRUARY THE IOWA coaches had a break. Aaron invited me to spend time with him in California, where he was staying in the off-season to work out. Shay and the baby were with him.

I stepped out to the curb at Los Angeles International Airport and spotted Aaron's white Audi. He rolled down the passenger's side tinted window—Shay was driving—and popped his face out: two big dimples and a radiant smile. As I neared the SUV, I could feel his happiness.

I got in the backseat and sat to the left of Avielle, who was buckled into her car seat. I couldn't stop looking at her and neither could Aaron. He constantly turned around to gaze at his three-month-old daughter. "Isn't she precious, D?" he said. "Isn't she the most beautiful princess you have ever seen? I am the luckiest man in the world."

We drove to a mall where there was a Macy's. Aaron told me to pick out a few shirts for work. I asked an employee where the sales rack was located, but Aaron stopped me. "It doesn't have to be off the sales rack like when we were kids," he said. "You're such a dork."

With my new shirts in a bag, we drove to their two-story rental home in Hermosa Beach. Shay showed me to my room and I took a shower. Once I was finished, I put on my jeans and one of the new shirts, and went into the living room. "Where's Aaron?" I asked Shay. She told me to check the roof.

I walked up the swirling staircase and opened the door. It was evening now, and in the dark distance I saw Aaron sitting at a table. There were small lights along the edge of the rooftop that created a relaxing orange glow. I moved toward Aaron.

Sitting alone, his eyes were focused on his lap. I took a seat next to him at the table. He was holding a gun.

I looked at him and his eyes met mine. He had a defeated look on his face. He turned his head straight forward, looking out past the roof lights, past the beach, and far away into the dark night over the Pacific Ocean. That was when I noticed one bullet lying on the table directly in front of him.

I was concerned for my brother. "What's wrong?" I asked.

He didn't answer. He kept staring straight ahead, like I wasn't there. I studied his face. It wasn't dark like it was during the Christmas photo; he appeared lost and sad.

"Aaron," I said quietly.

His eyes didn't move. He was in a different state, a different world. My voice couldn't snap him out of it.

He raised the gun from his lap and placed the tip under his chin, then slowly grazed the tip of the barrel back and forth from the edge of his chin to his Adam's apple. I was worried by how disconnected he appeared. He looked empty. I thought about touching him, but I was afraid because of the position the gun was in.

But I had to do something. I tenderly tapped him on the shoulder. "If you don't put the gun down, I'm going to go downstairs," I said.

I waited a few seconds and then stood up to leave. He reached for me with his left hand.

"D, stay," he said, placing the gun down on the table.

He looked at me and smiled softly—a smile that didn't reveal his dimples. It reminded me of the smile a stranger gives to another stranger when you accidentally make eye contact in passing. Only two hours earlier he had seemed like he was on top of the world. The sudden change in Aaron was staggering.

"Are you okay?" I asked.

"D, I'm fine," he said softly.

"Are you sure?"

"D, I'm fine," he said.

"Why do you have a gun?"

"People have guns, D," he said.

He said Shay should be dressed and ready to go out now—the babysitter had arrived when I had gotten out of the shower—and we needed to move downstairs. Aaron rose from his seat and I followed. I looked back at the gun and the bullet on the table, wondering if the gun was loaded.

From behind, I squeezed the back of Aaron's neck until he

flinched. This was something our father did to us as kids. Aaron turned at me and smiled as we descended the stairs.

EARLY THE NEXT MORNING, my brother's hands shook me awake. "D, I have to go to Florida," he said. "I'm leaving in a few minutes."

He had invited me to spend the entire week with him and now he was leaving less than twenty-four hours after I had landed. How could he forget that he was scheduled to fly across the country? Was this just the life of a high-profile NFL player?

I stayed in bed after he left the room until I heard footsteps scrambling around the house. I stepped out to watch him and it seemed like he didn't have the focus to keep up with what he was trying to achieve: gather enough belongings for a quick trip to Florida. He reminded me of a scattered child who didn't have his list of reminders directly in front of him.

I went back into my bedroom. Before Aaron left, he walked in to say good-bye and handed me a phone number. "D, if you need anything or want to do anything, give this number a call," he said. "This guy is a good guy and he's from the area. He will take care of you."

Aaron gave me a hug and a kiss on the cheek and then said, "I love you." At the door, he apologized repeatedly. "I don't want to leave but I have an appearance in Florida that I forgot about," he said. "I can't miss it."

I DIDN'T REMAIN UPSET for long. I attributed this to "Aaron being Aaron." If he didn't have a "to do" list written out he struggled with concentrating on the tasks he needed to achieve that day. I understood this about him—and was one of the things I loved about him. This was why I arranged a youth football camp around the weekend of my bachelor party, because it increased the odds of Aaron remembering to show up.

Aaron returned from Florida on my last night in Los Angeles. We went to a comedy club and afterward we spent the rest of the evening talking and laughing and sharing stories.

On the way to the airport, Aaron asked if I had enjoyed the previous night. "Aaron, it was perfect," I said. "It felt like we were kids again, just the two of us."

CHAPTER 24

APRIL 2013

I COULD FEEL MY MOTHER'S disappointment building through the phone. Two months after I visited my brother in California, Aaron had invited her down to Miami. She had just returned from her trip.

"At the airport I was greeted by a limo driver who was going to take me to the Fontainebleau Hotel," my mom said. "I sat in the limo excited to see my son. But I was also a little nervous, because I never knew which Aaron I would get. The good Aaron, the angry Aaron, or the disinterested Aaron.

"The hotel was beautiful. I walked inside and went to the front desk. Aaron forgot to show up and I wasn't going to hand over my credit card, because I couldn't put a balance that big on my card and Aaron was aware of that. The room he booked was around a thousand dollars a night for four nights. I was waiting in the lobby because they weren't going to let me into the room without a credit card on file. I had to beg the people who worked there to let me go in because my son wasn't there for me. Do you know how embarrassed I was? I didn't care about this uppity hotel or the damn limo ride. I could care less about that shit. I came here to see Aaron, and I didn't even see my son until the last night I was there.

"I was relaxing on the hotel bed, watching TV, when Aaron walks in the door with a designer book bag over his shoulder. Behind him are four goons with gold teeth and a stripper. He came over to me and gave me a kiss before sitting on the end of the bed near my feet. The other people were out on the balcony smoking and the prostitute lady was just sitting across the room in a chair.

"Aaron dropped his book bag off his shoulder, unzipped it, and poured all of his money out onto the bed we were on. He started counting it—it was a ton of money.

"I asked him, 'What is all this money for?' He said, 'I'm renting high-end cars for everyone.' We're talking like a Maserati, a Lamborghini, a Benz, and so on. They were in my room for about thirty minutes and then they all left."

Aaron returned to her hotel room the next morning, wearing the same clothes and stinking of booze. "He laid on the bed right next to me—he was so hungover."

She just kept saying, "Aaron, you were not raised like this."

He had already made arraignments for a limo driver to take her back to the airport, but now he offered to take her himself so they could spend more time together.

"No way in the world," she said. "At that point, I just wanted to go home. I was pissed."

Looking back on it later, she told me, "Over the years, all I ever wanted to do was be with Aaron and to see how he was doing, but at that time all I could see was how much he was changing. I thought it was all my fault. I would ask myself, *How could my baby turn out like this?*

"As much as I loved him and loved to see him, I started to hate being around him. As a parent, it is terrible seeing your child head down a path and not be able to do anything about it. I tried and I thought I would be able to help him, but he had stopped listening to me a long time ago."

"I MET YOUR BROTHER at a club called Greystone and from there we started hanging out," Ralph, one of Aaron's LA friends, told me. "I didn't notice anything out of the ordinary beside the fact that he came on to me one night. It was shocking to me but it didn't affect my friendship with him.

"Another time, we were in the bar at the Roosevelt Hotel and Aaron was coming on to a male bartender. I noticed it and Aaron saw that I noticed it. Aaron looked over at me and said, 'Please don't tell anybody.' We talked after and he said how it was so difficult for him being an NFL player, having a fiancée, and having a baby.

"One night we had strippers in a hotel room and I could tell Aaron wasn't entertained like I was. He just kind of sat there in his own world with a blank look on his face. I was like, 'What's up, dude?' And he said, 'Man, I'm not really into it.' I told him that we didn't need the strippers and we could have them leave. He told me that he was going along with it because he thought that was what I wanted.

"We walked out onto the patio to have a conversation. He said, 'I love Shay and my daughter and my family, but when it comes to my sexuality, I am really confused.' We then talked about him being open in the NFL. I thought that was the direction he was going in."

Another LA friend, Keith, described another evening at the Roosevelt. "Aaron was really fucked-up when I got there," he said. "Aaron was flirting with the male bartender. That night, Aaron was over-the-top with his flirting in public. I finally told him, 'Aaron, you can't do this shit here. This is Hollywood. You will be on TMZ in two days.' He looked at me without saying anything. It was for an entire minute he looked at me, a long eye exchange.

"I had called him out and he finally said, 'I ain't no faggot.'

"I asked him not to say that in front of me because I have gay friends—friends who are comfortable with their sexuality. I could tell that Aaron had a lot of self-conflict. Aaron was struggling to accept himself as a gay man."

CHAPTER 25

JUNE 2013

THREE WEEKS LATER, I was on a plane heading to One Patriot Place to complete a four-day internship. I had asked Iowa coach Kirk Ferentz if he could help me land an internship with an NFL team so I could continue to develop as a young coach. He made a few calls and days later I received an email from the Patriots inviting me to attend their offseason workouts. I was excited for two reasons: to learn and to see my brother.

A day after landing in Boston, I went to Aaron's house, where he was having a birthday party for Shay. I arrived in the afternoon. Aaron played the role of the gracious host: he talked to guests as he moved from the outdoor pool area—where I was seated with a dozen kids and adults—to the "Man Cave" downstairs. Aaron had a massive outside built-in grill, and I helped Aaron cook burgers and dogs for the group of twenty, which included Shay's sister and her boyfriend Odin Lloyd.

As I was cooking, Aaron jumped into the pool with his daughter, Avielle. I looked over the open grill lid and saw him guiding her around on a floaty in her pink sunglasses. It was beautiful watching them together.

We sang "Happy Birthday" to Shay and the group enjoyed a cake that Aaron and Shay had ordered for the special occasion. I walked downstairs, wanting to see if the pool table was available. Odin was there, sitting on a tall bar stool. We played a game. He was very friendly and soft-spoken. As I was chalking my pool stick, I heard my brother say from upstairs that a limousine would be picking everyone up later that night.

When the time came, about ten of us loaded into the limo for the ride to a club in downtown Boston, about forty-five minutes away from Aaron's. After taking our reserved seats on the stage and getting our drinks, we toasted Shay. For a few hours we enjoyed the music and danced.

Around 2 a.m. the limo took us back to Aaron's house. I went downstairs to the guest bedroom. Minutes later, I heard loud voices and bangs from the upper floor.

Thinking someone might have fallen, I jogged up the stairs. When I got to the living room, I looked up to the second-floor balcony and noticed there was a king-size mattress outside my brother's master bedroom, pressed up against the railing. Then I saw Shay's mother come out of the second-floor guest bedroom in her pajamas.

I walked up to the second floor. Shay's mom asked her daughter, who was standing in the doorway to her and Aaron's room, what was going on.

"Aaron can't find his cell phone," Shay said.

I wanted to talk to Aaron, but I sensed that something was going on between him and his fiancée. It wasn't the place to pry, so I called it a night.

Early the next morning I started packing my bags, excited to begin my internship. As I was making the bed, Aaron appeared at my bedroom door. He leaned his left shoulder against the trim in the doorway as he spoke.

"Good morning, D," he said.

"What happened with you last night?"

"I couldn't find my cell phone," he said.

"But Aaron, what *happened*? Your mattress was thrown in the hallway."

"Yeah, I know," Aaron said. "I need to work on that."

THE NEXT DAY, I walked into the team meeting room at One Patriot Place. I sat in the back of the auditorium and saw Tom Brady take a seat in the front row and his teammates fill in around him. When Aaron came in, he spotted me in the back and gave me an upbeat head nod and sat in his assigned chair. *Wow, my brother is a Patriot*, I thought.

Coach Belichick entered and stood behind the podium. I had a notebook, an orange and yellow highlighter, and three pens—I was worried about running out of ink—and I tried to write down every word he said.

"What type of improvements have you made as a player this off-season?" Belichick asked the team. "What type of player are you? Has your performance declined? Has your performance inclined? Are you a roller coaster? Are you consistent? . . . Do things right all the time. Be consistent."

I helped the quarterbacks and wide receivers coaches as needed. In staff meetings, I sat in a chair off to the side and against the wall; I was just thankful for the experience and I planned to take what I learned back with me to Iowa. One of my assignments was a red-zone study in which I analyzed the Patriots' most productive plays inside their opponents' twenty-yard line from the previous season.

One afternoon Aaron joined me in the tight ends' meeting room and together we continued studying the film. He shared with me everything he had been taught and the goal of each play. For a few minutes, it was like we were back in high school together.

The next day, I spotted Aaron during practice. He wasn't participating due to a shoulder injury and was walking behind the offensive huddle. He had such an angry look on his face. It was the Aaron of the failed Christmas photo, and it caused me to do a double take.

I immediately asked him, "Are you okay?"

He nodded and said, "Everything is cool."

I thought he was frustrated because he couldn't practice at full speed. We both carried on with work.

On my final day of the internship, I took a photograph of my locker and my nameplate that read D. HERNANDEZ. I then took a picture of Aaron's locker and his nameplate: A. HERNANDEZ.

On the plane ride back to Iowa, I couldn't stop looking at these pictures. I thought about how proud our dad would have been that his boys were together. Not only that, but for a few days at least, we were on the same team—the team Aaron grew up rooting for.

CHAPTER 26

JUNE 2013

On Saturday, June 15, my mother was scheduled to have breakfast with Aaron, Shay, and the baby. But when my mother arrived at Aaron's house, he was nowhere to be found. Around 11 a.m. Aaron and Odin Lloyd pulled into the driveway in a black Suburban, a vehicle that Aaron had rented. My mom saw Aaron hand Odin the keys.

"I don't need it," Aaron said to Odin. "Just bring it back to the rental car place on Monday."

Aaron was intoxicated. "Drunk as a skunk," my mom said. "He was wearing different clothes than what he went out in the previous night. He didn't come home."

The next day, June 16, was Father's Day. Aaron had a picnic with Shay and Avielle. When my mother asked him how it went, Aaron said he enjoyed the day. "The picnic was a stepping-stone in the right direction," my mom said. "I didn't think Aaron was the father he needed to be. He was always staying out late with his buddies and he wasn't treating Shayanna with enough respect."

Late in the workday the following Tuesday, I was sitting at my desk in Iowa City when my phone rang. It was Aaron.

Over the phone, I was a motormouth, going on about how much I enjoyed my internship with the Patriots.

Aaron finally interrupted. "D, will you please stop talking."

Something in the tone of his voice made me feel that something was terribly wrong—a brother's intuition. For a split second, I thought maybe something happened to our mother or our grandmother, or our father's twin brother, who had been battling cancer. Aaron continued.

"Listen," Aaron said, "Do you remember Odin?"

"Sure."

"Odin is dead," Aaron said. "I just want you to know, because you're my brother and I love you. He was found, and they're trying to investigate, and my name is being thrown around."

I felt frozen in my own body.

"So did you do it?"

"D, I swear on everything I didn't do it," he said.

He told me he couldn't talk and said, "I love you, D."

As soon as I hung up with Aaron, I couldn't get his words out of my mind. *Odin is dead. My name is being thrown around. Odin is dead. My name is being thrown around.*

I heard the nob to my office door begin to rattle as I saw it rotate before opening. One of the coaches on staff asked if everything was okay with my brother.

"What do you mean?" I asked.

He said he had just seen something about Aaron on television.

Surely, I thought, what Aaron had told me wasn't already making national news.

The coach left and shut the door. I grabbed a black rain jacket from my closet and placed it on the hook on the backside of my door, covering the one small window. I didn't want anyone to see my face.

I turned on the television. Then I saw the words crawling across the bottom of the screen:

POLICE ARE INVESTIGATING AARON HERNANDEZ IN CONNECTION WITH A POSSIBLE HOMICIDE. ODIN

LLOYD HAS BEEN FOUND SHOT TO DEATH IN AN INDUSTRIAL PARK NEAR HERNANDEZ'S HOUSE.

I wanted to hide. I wanted to disappear. But more than anything, I wanted to hug my brother and tell him everything would be all right.

As I tried to process what had happened, my mother called. All I could hear was her sobbing so hard that she was out of breath. "What did I do wrong?" she finally said.

I continued to try to comfort her. As I spoke, my phone beeped at least a dozen times—calls from concerned friends and family members, as well as reporters.

We hung up. I couldn't bear to watch any more television—Aaron's face was now on ESPN—so I turned it off. I removed the raincoat off the hook and peeked out my window to see if any coaches or players were nearby. It was all clear. I bolted out of my office, into the parking lot, and into my car.

That night I couldn't sleep. Tossing and turning, I prayed that my brother had nothing to do with Odin's death, that it was one big misunderstanding. I had no reason not to believe him.

I feared how Coach Kirk Ferentz would react to the news and how he would confront me the next day. I thought he might call me into his office and say, *We have to let you go. Our program can't be associated with the negative attention surrounding your brother.*

I wasn't sure if I would still have a job in a few hours. I couldn't believe how one short phone call could completely change my life.

The next morning, June 19, a Wednesday, my mom was getting ready for work in Bristol when Aaron called her.

"He said it would be nice if I could come to his house for support if I wanted to," my mom said. "I went to work and told my boss that I was going to Aaron's. On the drive there I had a knot in the pit of my stomach. I just knew that our lives would never be the same again. I just knew because it didn't add up. Something was wrong. I prayed to God that if Aaron was guilty and he really did this, that he would be put away."

As our mom neared Aaron's house, she saw about a dozen television trucks parked near his driveway. A news helicopter hovered above. A swarm of reporters and strangers stood in the street, gawking at the house. My mom squeezed through the crowd and went inside.

Aaron wasn't home; he was at the stadium with the team.

"Aaron called the house and asked me to come and pick him up," my mom said. "Once he came out and got in my car, I started asking him questions. As always Aaron said, 'Everything's going to be okay, Mom.' I drove to his house crying and placing my hand on his leg just above his knee, like I always did when I was driving with you boys."

I had to go home. That morning I explained the situation to Coach Ferentz and he couldn't have been more supportive, telling me to take as much time as I needed to be with my family. At the airport, it seemed like every television was tuned to a station that was showing pictures of my brother. I stood there staring at Aaron and then looked around and saw dozens of others stopped in their tracks by this breaking news.

A few days later, state police entered the front door of Aaron's house with search dogs to look for possible evidence. I watched it all on television from a friend's home in Connecticut. I wanted to be there with Aaron, but I knew I couldn't do anything for him. That time had passed. And I was worried about my face being plastered on television if cameras caught me exiting my car and walking into his home—the same thing that had happened to my mom.

As the police conducted their search, Aaron, Shay, Avielle, my mom, Shay's mom, and Shay's sister were ushered into the sunroom. They all sat in silence except for Aaron. "Aaron was acting like everything was perfectly fine," my mom said. "He made jokes and was his regular self."

That night my mom stayed at Aaron's. He brought her a small yellow bag of Lay's Classic potato chips and relaxed with her on the bed in a spare bedroom. They watched the news that was being broadcast from the front of Aaron's house as my mom rubbed Aaron's back.

She asked him if he was scared.

"I was, but not anymore, Mom," he said.

CHAPTER 27

JUNE 2013

Four days later, a Sunday, my mom left Aaron's home and drove back home to Bristol. She was convinced that this had all been a mix-up and that Aaron would not be arrested. She thought the only reason his name had been associated with Odin's death was that she saw Aaron hand Odin the keys to the black Suburban eight days earlier.

On the morning of June 26, a Wednesday, I went to the beach, hoping to escape everything for a few hours. But within minutes of placing my towel on the sand, my phone rang. It was my mother and she was screaming.

"They are taking him!" she said. "They are taking my baby. They are coming to arrest him!"

"I'm coming home now," I said.

I grabbed my sandals and ran to the car. I flipped the ignition and pushed the pedal to the floor with my bare foot. I wove through traffic on the highway, concerned about only one thing: reaching my mother, whose screams echoed in my ears the entire drive.

When I got to her house, my mom was clinging to the living room wall like she had no strength in her legs. I wrapped my arms around her before we settled on the couch to watch what was happening to Aaron.

The camera zoomed into Aaron's front door. Then it opened and I saw Aaron appear. He was wearing long red shorts that bounced a few inches lower than his kneecaps. His shoes were black, a low-cut training shoe. He had on a white short-sleeve V-neck T-shirt, but the sleeves just draped over the side of his body because his arms were not in them. His wrists were handcuffed behind his back as two detectives in dark suits directed him out onto his porch and toward a police car parked in his driveway.

We didn't know what would happen next. I sat in front of the television and watched the footage of my brother being hauled away in handcuffs again and again. It was a nightmare on repeat.

About an hour later, the live news coverage shifted to the inside of a Massachusetts courtroom, where Aaron was appearing for his arraignment. His lawyer put his hand on Aaron's shoulder as Aaron stood in front of the judge licking his lips, his eyes straight ahead.

"My baby, my baby, my baby," my mom kept saying as we watched. "I can't believe this is happening to my baby."

I turned up the television volume as the judge and the lawyers began talking.

"I'm going to be sick," my mom said and left the living room.

I could hear her dry-heave in the bathroom as my eyes remained focused on the screen.

A bald man stepped to the podium in the courtroom. "Your honor, the defendant is charged with the murder of Odin Lloyd," the assistant district attorney said.

I was horrified.

About two hours later a camera showed a white van carrying Aaron to jail. He got out of the van, his arms now in the sleeves of his white V-neck T-shirt. I kept my eyes on Aaron, because I didn't know when I would be able to see him again.

THE NEXT DAY WAS a blur of events: Aaron was denied bail. His silver Toyota 4Runner was towed out of Tanya's garage and was linked to an entirely different case, the 2012 drive-by double murder of Daniel de Abreu and Safiro Furtado in the South End of Boston.

Reporters repeatedly knocked on our door on Greystone Avenue throughout the afternoon and into the evening. When we didn't answer, they dropped their business cards on the front steps. By sundown, the steps were covered with cards.

At one point my mother and I went out to our backyard. A man approached, claiming to be a friend of my father. He offered his condolences and then began peppering us with questions. My mom started to answer—she didn't understand that this man was actually a reporter and didn't know our family—until I told her to stop when I noticed him pulling a recording device out of his left pocket.

Another reporter offered us Subway sandwiches in return for a few comments.

My mom hadn't slept in days—dark purple bags had formed around her exhausted eyes. We needed to go to the grocery store, so we waited until our street was clear of press. Once the reporters had called it a night, we hurried to our car and drove off.

Once inside Price Chopper, I grabbed a ticket at the deli line and waited for my number to be called. The deli clerk turned to me and said, "I saw on TV that you were arrested. How did you get out of jail?"

I stared at the clerk, unable to speak. My mom was speechless as well. I clenched my jaw, said nothing about her mistake, and we walked out of the grocery store empty-handed.

My high school coach called. "Do you want to go out to dinner?"

"That would be great," I said. "I would love to. I need some fresh air." I accepted his offer to pick me up.

I went to the basement and found one of my father's black baseball hats in a storage bin—I never wore hats—and pulled the brim low before I walked down the driveway and got into my coach's car. I told him we should go to a restaurant that had dim lighting. I didn't want to be recognized by anyone.

Sitting in a corner away from the other customers, we ate chicken wings and I tried to make small talk—but I couldn't. I could see my coach's lips moving, yet I couldn't focus on what he was saying. My mind was overwhelmed with one image: Aaron being led out of his house and into the police cruiser.

After dinner, my coach dropped me off at a friend's house. I needed company. We had several cold beers and then I felt myself breaking down. I went outside and, alone in the dark, sat against the side of his house. I cried and cried and cried.

Brian Ferentz had told me to reach out to him if I needed anything at any time. In need of someone now, I called him.

"How are you doing?" he asked.

I couldn't talk. I sobbed into the phone, and he patiently listened for a few minutes. Eventually I gathered myself and thanked him for answering and said I was sorry for calling.

"I'm so sorry, DJ," Brian said. "There is no need to apologize to me. Feel free to call me anytime."

CHAPTER 28

JULY 2013

I WANTED MY OLD LIFE BACK.

A week after Aaron was arrested, one of my aunts in Bristol had a birthday party. Even with my own family, I became more guarded, more closed off. I would ask myself, *Is it okay to be openly supportive of my brother? Is that right? Does that make me a cold person?* I walked into the banquet hall and stood in the back, assessing the room. Music was playing, family members were dancing, and others were conversing at tables.

After my aunt's birthday party, I asked a friend out to eat at a local diner. She said yes. My cousin Jay and two of his friends—Todd and Alan—came along as well.

As soon as we entered the diner, I felt every set of eyes shift in my direction. I put my head down. The hostess said, "I am so sorry about your brother," and led us to a booth in the back corner. As I walked past the filled tables, I heard the whispers grow louder. "That's Aaron's brother," one guy said. "That's Aaron's brother."

The five of us took our seats. "I don't care if people say shit to me," I said, "I am not getting involved. Remember that: I am not getting involved." I knew if I got into a fight, it would make national news and I would lose my job at Iowa. Coaching was the only thing I had. It was my lifeline.

As we were reading the menu, two strangers at a nearby table stood up and started walking toward us.

One of them said, "Hey, DJ, how's your brother?" He started laughing. I turned to everyone at the table. "Remember what I said."

The two guys stood over the end of our table and began making the sound of machine guns with their lips and slapping each other on the back like they had just come up with the joke of the year.

My cousin turned to them and said, "Guys, DJ's had a hard enough week as it is. Can you just leave us alone? We don't want any trouble."

They laughed again and started making more machine-gun sounds. Todd, one of my cousin's friends, looked at them in disgust. "That's not even funny," he said. "It's immature. How old are you guys?"

Just then, one of the strangers wound his right hand back and slapped Todd's hat off his head, causing it to fly across the table. Todd rose to his feet and tackled the stranger. Jay jumped over the table and onto the second guy as they both began to gang up on Todd. Alan was walking back from the bathroom and ran at one of the aggressors, driving his shoulder into him, sending him to the ground.

Still sitting in my seat, I saw Alan in a chokehold getting smashed in the face, fist after fist.

"DJ!" Alan yelled to me. "Help me, damn it!"

I shook my head, telling him no. I felt like the biggest coward, but I couldn't risk losing my job at Iowa. Alan escaped the headlock, grabbed a ketchup bottle off the table, and rifled it at one of the guys who was charging toward him. He dodged the bottle, but it popped a customer in the head, dropping her to the ground.

"She's dead!" another customer screamed. It appeared that the lady who was knocked out on the ground had blood covering her face, but it was the ketchup that had splattered everywhere.

As soon as I saw an opening, I walked out of the diner with my friend. It looked like a tornado had ripped through: tables were torn from the walls and overturned, booth cushions were spread across the floor, and plates of food and silverware were scattered on the ground. As the two of us drove away from the diner, I saw police cruisers rushing into the parking lot.

The next morning, I went to my cousin's house to make sure everyone was okay. Approaching the backyard, I saw my cousin's friends sitting on the picnic table, still wearing what they had on the night before. They had bruises and cuts on their faces, their clothes were ripped and dotted with dried blood, and their knuckles were swollen.

"You look rested," Alan said sarcastically to me.

"I told you before it all started that I was not going to get involved," I said.

"I was getting slammed in the head right in front of you and you just shook your head no and sat there?"

"I told you I wasn't getting involved," I repeated.

My cousin turned to Alan and Todd and said, "Enough, guys. If DJ had thrown one punch, it would have been national news because of Aaron's situation." To me he said, "You did the right thing, D."

His friends didn't agree. They shook their heads in disgust and limped inside.

A few hours later I was back at my mother's home when my iPhone rang. It was a local reporter. "Can you please comment about the brawl you were involved in?" he asked.

I hung up the phone without saying a word and quickly called Coach Kirk Ferentz to tell him what had happened and that I had stayed out of the fight. "I don't want to lose my job and I had nothing to do with it," I said.

"You did the right thing, DJ," Coach Ferentz said. "I appreciate you calling. There is no need to worry. Be safe and let me know if you need anything."

That was impossible: I worried about everything, all the time.

CHAPTER 29

JULY 2013

On the fourth of July, my mother hosted a family barbecue at her house. I sat next to Shayanna and held Aaron's eight-month-old daughter. I didn't want to let go. I thought about how innocent she was and what effect everything would have on her as she grew older if my brother remained incarcerated. She was Aaron's pride and joy but had no way of knowing it.

My mom went inside for a few minutes and then came running out the back door with her phone in hand. "It's Aaron!" she yelled. "It's Aaron!"

I handed Avielle back to Shayanna and followed my mother around the backyard as she spoke to Aaron, waiting for my turn. She gave me the phone. I needed to know how Aaron was holding up.

I was surprised by the tone of his voice. He sounded upbeat. "I'm doing great," he said. "I have to stay positive, D."

He asked me to put him on speakerphone. With eight of us huddled close, he asked how Avielle was doing. Then we heard an automated voice say, "You have one minute." The prison timed his calls. We quickly said our good-byes and Aaron was gone again.

One week later, on July 11, my mom and I visited Aaron for the first time. That morning, sitting in our childhood bedroom, I put on my outfit—the prison had a strict dress code. I never hated putting on nice clothes so much in my life. I tried to imagine how different things would be if our father were still alive. I heard my mother crying as she dressed in her room.

I was afraid to see Aaron. For weeks, I'd type his name in my computer search browser because I still struggled to believe he was in this mess. It didn't seem real; I needed proof. It was like I had become a motivational speaker for myself. I needed to reassure myself that I could keep my emotions in check while visiting my brother in the worst place imaginable.

At just past 8 a.m., my mother and I got in her Nissan Juke and headed to the Bristol County Sheriff's Office in North Dartmouth, Massachusetts.

My mother parked the car outside the facility. We entered the lobby of the jail and filled out forms requesting to see Aaron. The waiting room was dark and filled with corrections officers. I sat down and avoided eye contact with anyone.

An officer asked me, "Are you here for Hernandez?" he said. "Gosh, you look just alike."

We placed our belongings in a small orange locker. I looked at the other visitors and wondered what their stories were. Were they as broken as I was?

Waiting to enter the visiting area, my mother whispered to me. "How did our lives change so much?"

They called our names. We walked over to the corrections officers and were patted down before being led into a small stall, where we would meet with my brother. There were two steel stools bolted side by side, about two feet apart. I took a seat on the left stool, my mother on the right. The stools were cold and uncomfortable. I didn't want to touch anything.

For several minutes, my mother and I waited without speaking. A glare reflected off the glass into our faces, making it hard to see through to the other side, where my brother would eventually be sitting.

We heard a few loud bangs coming from somewhere out of view. My body grew tense. It was like I was meeting my brother for the first time. An officer led Aaron to the glass. I struggled to see his face as I moved my head to the left and then to the right, trying to find a clear line of sight. Aaron started laughing at me. He could see us perfectly from his seat. All I could see was a silhouette of his head.

My mother grabbed the phone off the wall and held it between us. The silver cord was short and stiff, so I had to lean to the right edge of my stool to get my ear to the phone. It was quiet at first, and I didn't know what to say. Aaron's voice went in and out, like we had poor reception. So my mother hung up the phone and we talked the best we could through the glass.

Aaron was thrilled that we took the time to visit him. He was convinced that everything was in God's hands. In college he had *In God's Hands* tattooed on his right forearm.

There were so many things I wanted to say to Aaron but I knew I couldn't. Getting mad at him wouldn't do any good for any of us. So at first I sat there simply looking at his face, trying to read how he was feeling. He started smiling and cracking jokes like he did when we were younger. It was almost like he went back to the kid I knew on Greystone Avenue, sitting across from me at the dinner table making me smile as we completed our homework assignments.

I stood up to get a clear view of him. He did the same. Now I saw him, and I noticed his face shift. I felt his sadness, like he knew this was his new reality. I could tell it was a side of him that he didn't want us to see because he quickly snapped out of it. He said something funny and I started joking around, too, telling him amusing stories about anything I could think of, trying to get him to smile and to get my mind off this tragic situation. I wanted him to be able to close his eyes and have something positive to think about back in his prison cell, isolated and alone.

Visiting hours ended. This was going to be the last time I would see him before I traveled back to Iowa, and I didn't know when I'd be in a room with him again. Since our father passed, we never said good-bye to each other—it was too concrete. So I said, "I love you. I'll see you later."

As Aaron walked out of the room, I tried to freeze the image of him through the glass in my mind. I didn't want to let go.

CHAPTER 30

FALL 2013

I flew back to Iowa. I found a thick stack of sympathy cards stuffed in my mailbox, which I read at my desk. I was reminded again of what I wanted to forget—my brother was in jail.

There were times I would walk past a TV in the lobby that was tuned to ESPN and hear commentators talking about Aaron's downward spiral.

Shortly after returning, a few recruits and their families were touring the facility. ESPN was on again and the topic was my brother. I ran into our recruiting coordinator's office and asked if we should change the channel on the television, because I didn't want them to think negatively about the university.

Three days a week, I jogged around campus, and I started getting texts from friends asking how my run was going? I later found out that people had been tweeting that Aaron Hernandez's brother was jogging through campus. I couldn't outrun the reality even in Iowa.

I was worried that my tight ends wouldn't respect me anymore or that they would be afraid of me because of everything my brother was involved in, so one afternoon I called all six of them into my office. I stood in front of them and said, "My brother's situation has nothing to do with us as a team. We must dominate this season."

"Coach," one of the players said, "we have your back."

Our season flew by. We finished 8-5 and lost in the Outback

Bowl to LSU, 21–14. My brother tried to watch as many of our games as he could, and I always looked forward to discussing our performance with Aaron.

I had been dating a girl in Iowa for several months. After the season, for her birthday, we went to Formosa restaurant near campus with her sister and her sister's fiancé.

We were seated at a table, which faced a floor-to-ceiling window. Midway through our meal I noticed a group of people outside on the sidewalk stop in their tracks and point at me. They pretended to shoot and kill each other and fall to the ground dead. My body turned stiff and our conversation turned awkward.

After dinner, we moved to a nearby bar for a nightcap. As I stood inside, a few people approached me and asked how it felt to be a murderer's brother.

I told my girlfriend, "I'm outta here."

I rode in a taxi to my apartment at 906 Benton Avenue. I entered the door, threw my Christmas tree to the other side of the living room, and walked to the kitchen. I grabbed the largest knife from my wooden knife block and stormed into the bathroom.

I turned the light on and stared at myself in the mirror. It was like I was seeing past myself into a dark place. I visualized pushing the knife through my chest. I tightened my grip with my right hand, squeezing the knife so hard that my fingernails were pressing into my palm, nearly causing it to bleed. I was ready to end the pain. I was convinced that the blade was my escape, my only answer.

I extended my right arm away from my body before bringing it back into my chest. My hand nicked the bottom of the mirror, and like that, I snapped out of the dark world I was in, like I woke up from a blackout. I remember seeing my cheeks covered with tears in the mirror. I dropped the knife into the sink and stumbled into my bedroom, where I sat on the floor, rocking back and forth.

After a while, I called my mother. She answered, but I couldn't talk. I just sighed heavily into the phone over and over and over.

"Are you okay, DJ?" she asked.

I didn't respond.

"D, what is wrong?" she asked.

"I can't take this anymore, Mom," I said, as I cried uncontrollably.

"You've got to go to counseling, DJ," she said. "I went and it helped me. You've got to go."

Instead of attending class the next Monday—I was working on a second master's—I drove to the campus counseling department. In the parking garage, I pulled the hood of my black Iowa sweatshirt over my head because I didn't want anyone to recognize me. I didn't want to appear damaged or weak or as if I couldn't handle what was going on in my life.

I walked up a flight of stairs and into the counseling office. I filled out paperwork but didn't sign my name, afraid someone would call it out loud. As I sat in a chair with my head buried in a magazine, one of the counselors came to the waiting area and asked if she could help me. I said yes and followed her into her office.

I told her I couldn't think for myself, I couldn't focus, and I couldn't control the negative thoughts attacking me. It was like something had taken control over my mind and was continuing to pump it with the worst images from my life.

After speaking a short while, she explained that after my third individual session I would have to transition to group counseling. There was no way that was happening. I feared word getting out on social media that "Aaron Hernandez's brother has entered counseling." I thanked the counselor for her time and left the office.

I found a different counselor who could meet with me first thing in the morning. I had never lied to our offensive coordinator or head coach before, but now I told the staff I had a morning class. I didn't want them to know I was seeking help.

During our first session I remained closed off; there was no chance I was going to tell him how I had almost ended my life a few nights before. But over time I began to open up about Aaron and the negative thoughts I had. I explained how it felt like every person I was close to had left me—my dad, my ex-wife, and now my brother. I began to push everyone in my life away, because I didn't want to take the chance of getting hurt again. It was a relief to let all of this out.

After a few weeks, I had hope for better days and for a dramatic change in my life, a change I needed personally. It was the start of a long process of finding balance and overcoming my depression. The books my counselor recommended for me—*The Secret*, *The Four Agreements*, *The Fifth Agreement*, and *The Mastery of Love*—were the same books Aaron was beginning to read in prison.

CHAPTER 31

JANUARY 2015

ON THE MORNING OF January 19, I exited the elevator at the Justice Center in Fall River, Massachusetts. Today was a big day: the beginning of opening statements in Aaron's trial.

Wearing a gray sport coat, a button-down shirt, and dress pants, I pulled opened the courtroom door. As I neared the front of the room, I saw a lady in a blue dress—Odin Lloyd's mom. My heart broke for her and the entire Lloyd family.

I sat in the first wooden bench on the left side of the courtroom, six feet behind where Aaron and his defense team would be stationed. For several minutes, I rocked back and forth, my nerves on edge. I looked at the empty seats that would be filled by the jury and watched the prosecution organize their notes.

Aaron entered the room. The first thing I noticed were the tattoos on his hands—tattoos he had dating back to college that from a distance looked like different shades of black ink. I wondered what the jurors' first impression of my brother would be when they saw him. Aaron was big with broad shoulders and still looked like he could play in the NFL; he had kept in shape during his nineteen months of incarceration.

Before Aaron took his seat next to one of his defense attorneys, Charles Rankin, he looked back at our family section—I was there with our mom, Jeff, Shayanna, our uncle David, and our aunt Lisa. Aaron mouthed the words "I love you" and "Thank you." He sat down.

Judge E. Susan Garsh appeared and the jurors filed in. It was now time for the prosecution to give opening statements.

The Bristol County prosecutor Patrick Bomberg said that Aaron orchestrated Lloyd's murder and was the triggerman. The state laid out what it believed happened in the early-morning hours of June 17, 2013, presenting a timeline:

On June 16, after having dinner and drinks with a few friends, Aaron returned home. He texted two other friends—Ernest "Bo" Wallace and Carlos "Charlie Boy" Ortiz—and they drove from Bristol to Aaron's house. Aaron had met Bo through Tanya years earlier and had only recently started spending time with Carlos. Both Bo and Carlos had criminal records.

The three of them then picked up Lloyd just after 2:30 a.m. and drove to a secluded industrial park less than a mile from Aaron's home. The prosecution claimed that Lloyd had recently said something to Aaron that had angered him and caused Aaron to lose trust in Lloyd. Because of this, the prosecution said, Aaron fatally shot Lloyd six times.

Video surveillance showed a Nissan Altima, which was rented in Aaron's name, outside of Lloyd's house at 2:33 a.m. About an hour later, more video surveillance revealed Aaron, Bo, and Carlos returning to Aaron's house without Lloyd in the car. A text message that Lloyd sent to his sister indicated he was with someone he referred to as "NFL" before he was killed.

The prosecutor also presented an image from Aaron's personal home surveillance system that revealed Aaron carrying a dark-shaped object in his hands as he stood in his front foyer. The prosecution alleged that it was the Glock used in the killing of Lloyd. They went on to allege that the gun was disposed of by Shay the next day. (Shay was charged with perjury, but the charge was eventually dropped.)

Aaron's lawyers went next.

"Aaron Hernandez is an innocent man," said Michael Fee, one of Aaron's lawyers. "The evidence will show that Aaron Hernandez did not murder his friend Odin Lloyd, nor did he ask or orchestrate anyone else to murder him. Aaron Hernandez is not guilty. We are here because the police and prosecutor targeted Aaron from the very beginning. As soon as they found out that Aaron Hernandez, the celebrity football player, the New England Patriot, was a friend of Odin Lloyd's, it was over. Aaron never had a chance."

After the opening statements, Judge Garsh gave the jury instructions. "The commonwealth is not required to prove that the defendant himself performed the act that caused Odin Lloyd's death," she said. "However, to establish the defendant is guilty of murder, the commonwealth must prove two things beyond a reasonable doubt. First, the commonwealth must prove that the defendant knowingly participated in the commission of that crime and, second, the commonwealth must prove that he did so with the intent required to commit that crime."

Walking out of the courtroom after the first day, I was torn. The timeline and information the prosecutors presented raised questions about what happened on that early morning. And when they showed Aaron with what looked like a gun in his front foyer, I felt a punch to the gut. I knew that any picture of my brother holding a gun was not going to help his case. It looked bad, but I needed more information.

For the first few days of the trial I sat in the courtroom and hoped the jurors were not like my mother, who believed Aaron was probably guilty before the trial even started because of all the negative articles she had read about him. All I wanted was for the jurors to have open minds and determine the case based on the facts presented, not what had been previously reported in the media. But I understood that was going to be difficult to do, because of the extensive coverage Aaron's case had received from the moment his name was first tied to Odin's death.

After several days of sitting behind Aaron, I had to return to work in Iowa. But my heart never left Aaron's side, and my mind never left the courtroom.

A few nights later, in my Iowa City apartment, I dropped to my knees, said my nightly prayers, and climbed into bed. Exhausted from the day of work—and the mental energy I expended keeping up with the trial—I quickly drifted asleep.

The places I went in my sleep haunted me.

I'm standing on the gravel in the industrial park, headlights blinding my eyes. Cold and nervous, I don't know what to do as a man points a gun directly at me. I sense death coming.

Shots are fired at me—blasts that echo through the darkness as bullets rip through my skin.

As I lie on the gravel, my neck grows weak and then I'm paralyzed. Pain courses through me as I feel the heat radiating from each gunshot wound. I taste blood coating the back of my throat. Tears stream down my cheeks as the headlights of the car back away, driving off into the night.

The smaller the taillights become, the more hopeless I am. Who will save me? How can I survive? My breathing becomes labored. As I lie here next to a white towel, my eyes grow heavy and close.

Then I feel a warm and familiar hand grab my arm. My spirits are lifted. I am transported to Aaron's house. Suddenly, I am Aaron and my fiancée, Shayanna, is crying as she holds Avielle. Shay refuses to let go of my arm.

A police officer places my hands together behind my back, snapping the handcuffs tight. I duck into the backseat of the cop car. I try to look out the window, but my knees are pressed against the driver's seat, making it nearly impossible to move.

I squeeze my eyelids shut, hoping this nightmare will end, but noises distract me. Voices bark from the police radio, a siren sounds, and the car vibrates from the thrum of the helicopter hovering above. I become light-headed.

Now the doors open, and now I flash in and out of characters: I am Odin, I am Aaron, I am Bo, I am Carlos.

I feel someone shaking me—it is my mother snapping me out of this terrifying dream.

When I actually woke up, I was alone in Iowa City, my body and my entire bed soaked with sweat.

Different versions of this dream tormented me nightly. The explicit details and the clear, cinematic quality of the visions made me afraid to fall asleep. I had become obsessed with the trial, thinking about it all day, and now I was living in it within my nightmares.

DURING THE TRIAL, I asked a girl named Karen out on a date. I first saw her at a mall near campus where she worked in a retail store. Hesitant to approach while she was working, I contacted her over social media. I eventually asked her out to dinner and was delighted when she said yes. But on the designated night, as I was grabbing my coat from the closet to go meet her, she texted to cancel.

Two months later, as the trial was nearing its end, she texted and gave me a second chance, with one stipulation: she wanted to bring a coworker.

At first I thought she was joking, but then I realized I was the only one laughing on the phone. After our call ended, I put myself in her shoes and thought: *Would I do the same thing?*

The three of us had a wonderful dinner. The conversation flowed naturally and I thought there was a chance that this might lead to another date. Walking Karen to her car afterward, I asked why she had canceled our first date.

"I enjoyed our phone conversation and was really looking forward to dinner, but when I told my coworkers about a date with you, everyone started to panic," she said. "I had no idea who you were related to and initially I had no idea who Aaron was. Then my boss came to me and said, 'Out of all of the guys in Iowa, you choose to go on a date with Aaron Hernandez's brother?' I just needed more time to think."

I understood and hugged her before she got into her car.

Back home, I fiddled with my phone, not knowing if I should text her. I didn't want to appear clingy. But then I felt my phone vibrate. It was a text from Karen.

"I had a really good time," she wrote.

Excited, I gave myself a little fist pump and said aloud, "Victory!"

CHAPTER 32

APRIL 15, 2015

It began as a normal Wednesday morning at the University of Iowa. I attended an 8 a.m. staff meeting. But as I sat in a corner of the conference room, I kept glancing at my phone, hoping to receive a text that the jury had reached a verdict.

During the trial Aaron and I spoke at least once a week over the phone. We never discussed the details of the case, because Aaron knew his calls were recorded and was afraid anything he said could be taken out of context. But in his letters he expressed optimism about his innocence being proven.

I knew it could go either way—it all depended on how the jury interpreted the evidence. Still, I had been confused from the opening statements. I didn't understand how four guys could go into an industrial park and how the three who left would have different charges brought against them. Aaron's charges were more severe than Bo's and Carlos's, in spite of no murder weapon being found or surveillance showing who actually pulled the trigger.

The meeting at Iowa ended. I walked to my desk, which was in an open area clustered with eight other desks. As I approached my space, I looked at the television on my desk, tuned to a news channel. A scroll on the bottom read: "The jury in the Aaron Hernandez trial has reached a verdict."

My heart jackhammered. The television switched to the courtroom, where I saw my brother standing with his lawyers by his side as he waited for the jury's decision. I couldn't take my eyes off him, praying the jury would announce a "not guilty" finding. Then the words were read by the jury foreperson.

"Guilty of murder in the first degree."

Everything fell silent. I was numb.

I stared at Aaron on the screen. When he heard the words "guilty of murder in the first degree," I saw him deflate and thought he was going to fall. He was in shock, I felt it. He turned to my mother and Shay, who had their hands over their faces, sobbing, their bodies shaking. Aaron mouthed, "Be strong."

It felt like my own life was over. I tried to hold myself together but then I couldn't suppress the emotion. Tears rolled down my cheeks. I felt hands pat me on the back and heard someone asking me if I needed to take a walk.

But I couldn't. It would have felt like I was leaving my brother, so I continued to watch the television, continued to cry with my hands on the side of my head like a horse wearing blinders. I knew this meant that Aaron might never be free again.

Coach Kirk Ferentz came to me and placed his hands around my shoulders and whispered into my ear, "If you need anything or need to take time off to be with your family, just let me know."

I kept thinking of my mother, who had driven by herself to the courthouse for the first time that morning—the family members she usually went with couldn't attend. Now I worried that she wouldn't have anyone to be with as she made her way home on the two-hour drive.

I called my mother as she was waiting for the elevator outside the courtroom, but she said she couldn't talk. I told her I loved her.

After I hung up, I saw the TV cameras bombard her as she pushed through the heavy courthouse doors to leave.

I gave her a few minutes to get to her car and called her again to ask if she was okay to drive home.

"I'm okay, D," she said. "How are you?"

I didn't have the strength to respond. For what seemed like five minutes, there was silence between us.

Finally, she said, "You're going to be okay."

I started crying again.

I somehow attended an 11:15 a.m. coaches meeting—I don't remember one word that was said—and then I finally took a walk. I went downstairs to the coaches' locker room to be alone, trying to clear my head and balance my emotions.

I looked up at a television in the locker room, tuned to ESPN, and saw commentators talking about my brother and his case. They kept going on and on about the $40 million contract he had signed and how Aaron had everything but threw it all away.

I heard the door to the locker room open. I tried to bury my head deeper into my locker, hoping to look preoccupied.

Coach Ferentz approached me again. "I've been trying to find you," he said.

I looked at him, but I couldn't find any words to say.

"DJ, I can't imagine the pain you and your mother are feeling right now. I'm so sorry and I am here for you if you need anything. Hang in there."

Crying, I stammered, "Coach, would you mind if I go home for the day? I'm just so exhausted right now and I need to be alone."

"Of course," he said with kindness in his voice. "Just don't do anything stupid, and make sure you touch base with me in the morning."

As I drove to my apartment, I wondered what Aaron was thinking.

CHAPTER 33

SUMMER 2015

This would be the first time I would be seeing Aaron since he was convicted and sent to Souza-Baranowski Correctional Center, located in Lancaster, Massachusetts. It was a rare contact visit, and I wondered if I would be able to hug my brother.

After clearing the security checkpoint with other visitors, I walked through the green bulletproof doors and then down a long narrow hallway. Along the right side of the white walls, through the windows, I could see the barbed-wire fence and an outdoor picnic table that sat alone in the sunshine. The sky was blue on this August morning, and I wondered if I was going to meet Aaron out there at the picnic table. I had no idea; I was just following the few visitors walking in front of me who seemed to have experience with the contact-visit protocol.

An officer opened another door and guided us into a large open room filled with chairs lined in long rows facing each other. Four officers roamed the area. I watched inmates enter and embrace their loved ones.

Then Aaron entered the room and our eyes met. We both lit up. As soon as Aaron was close to me, I looked at the officer who was escorting him to see if it was okay for me to hug him. He nodded. We embraced and then sat down.

We were directly across from each other, four feet apart, a blue line of tape on the floor between us. For the first few minutes we didn't say much; it was like we were two shy people trying to make conversation. It took time for me to process the entire scene and comprehend that this was where Aaron would spend the rest of his life.

Aaron asked me if I liked his outfit—he was wearing a gray prison uniform—and his watch, which he wore on his left wrist and featured a thin black silicone band with a small digital face. He showed me his all-white prison-issued shoes and told me he had cleaned them to look fresh for my visit. His prison clothes looked ironed and pressed—his shirt and pants were wrinkle-free. He'd recently gotten a haircut.

"How are you doing, Aaron?"

"You know. Every day is the same."

He was much calmer and less talkative than the last time I had seen him in prison, eight months earlier. It was like his body was recovering from the shock of the verdict four months ago. He seemed heartbroken and internally wounded.

I leaned in to Aaron as close as I could without going over the blue line. I had to ask my brother if he did it. We both knew his letters were monitored and his phone calls were reviewed, so I knew he couldn't fully open up about what transpired the night Odin was killed. But now it was just brother in front of brother. I needed to hear his answer in person, face-to-face, eyes to eyes, without glass separating us. I needed to know Aaron's truth.

"What the fuck happened that night?" I quietly asked.

Aaron shook his head slowly for several seconds, back and forth, back and forth until my head started moving along with his rhythm. Then he whispered, "It's craaaaaaaazy."

He was getting more upset as we looked into each other's eyes.

"Aaron, I'm your brother and I love you no matter what," I said. "I need to know: Did you kill Odin?"

With tears welling in his eyes, in a voice no louder than a whisper, he said, "Drugs will fuck you up, but not fuck you up enough to kill someone. I didn't do it, D. I did not do it."

CHAPTER 34

My time as a graduate assistant coach was expiring and I was about to be out of a job. Unable to find another coaching opportunity, I packed my life into a U-Haul and left the beauty of Iowa City. For fifteen hours I drove south across the plains until I reached Dallas, Texas, where one of the Hawkeye coaches had a connection with a local roofing and remodeling company. They had a sales position available and I accepted. Still in the beginning phases of our relationship, Karen stayed back in Iowa City, but we vowed to continue a long-distance relationship. It was time for a new beginning.

I moved into an apartment. The challenge of starting over—and leaving the true love of my life, football—was nerve-racking. Besides lemonade sales as a kid with Aaron, I didn't have any sales experience.

After a few months, I started a company called High Rise Roofing and Remodeling. Shortly after, a massive hailstorm pounded the Dallas–Fort Worth Metroplex. I was about to perform a roof inspection when the storm hit. I quickly climbed down my ladder as hailstones the size of golf balls hammered the ground.

Within hours, I had dozens of homeowners calling me, panicked by the hail that had blasted through their roofs, smashed through their windows, and ripped apart their siding. As I drove through the pitch-black neighborhood—the power was out in this section of the city—my headlights beamed onto cars that were flattened as if massive oaks had fallen on top of them. Shards of glass were everywhere, covering streets, sidewalks, and lawns.

I parked my truck and worked with others to tarp roofs. Then the rain began to fall and it became too slippery for us to maintain our traction. With a flashlight in hand, I inched down off the roof and down the ladder. We then boarded up windows and swept up glass.

Helping others lifted me out of my funk; these new relationships gave me a sense of purpose again. I relished sitting in living rooms with families, drinking coffee and listening to them talk about their lives and the progress they were making in returning to normalcy after the storm.

IN JANUARY 2016, I flew with Karen back to Bristol to introduce her to my mother and Aaron for the first time. After arriving at the prison in Massachusetts, we stepped out of the car and proceeded toward the front entrance. Holding hands, our grip was firm as we walked alongside the barbed-wire fence.

"Are you sure you want to do this?" I asked.

"I'm ready," she said.

An officer met us in the waiting area and directed us through a doorway and into the visiting room. We sat down and I rubbed Karen's knee, trying to ease her discomfort. Sitting upright, she was as stiff as a board. Then a buzzer sounded and Aaron walked in. Karen didn't know what to do or say, so she just looked at me—even as Aaron was looking at her with his big smile.

Aaron asked Karen how she was doing. She turned her head toward him and said, "I'm fine." Then she smiled.

Aaron and I started talking as Karen watched. She didn't know what to say, but she later told me that she had no idea that Aaron and I had such a strong bond, that we could effortlessly pick up a conversation as if we'd never been apart. She noted that we had the same hand gestures, facial expressions, and the same crease in our small foreheads when we laughed.

At one point Aaron pulled out his fake front teeth and started smiling. We all laughed because he was so goofy.

The visit lasted an hour. As Karen and I got in our car, I asked her what she thought.

"The time went so fast," she said. "I wanted to bottle it up. I saw so much love and emotion. I'll never forget that."

CHAPTER 35

OCTOBER 2016

Tanya Singleton—our cousin who was the person that Aaron confided in the most—was incarcerated for refusing to testify before the grand jury investigating the death of Odin Lloyd. After spending a few months in jail, she pleaded guilty to criminal contempt and was placed on house arrest.

She was suffering from stage 4 metastatic breast cancer. My mother and Jeff remained distant from Tanya, and my mother continued to seethe. "I thought Tanya was brainwashing Aaron to be against me all those years," my mom said. "She never said no to him and she would allow Aaron to do anything he wanted. She didn't teach him anything or discipline him. Instead, she would accept anything he wanted to do."

In October 2015 Tanya passed away in a bed that was set up in her living room. After she died, my mom spoke to Aaron and noted that "karma is a bitch," that Tanya's death was payback for her past actions. Aaron was deeply hurt by the comment, and he wrote her several stinging letters, spelling out the pain it caused him.

One year later, my mother felt uneasy during her two-hour car drive to Lancaster, Massachusetts.

"I really didn't want to go," she said. "I hated seeing Aaron in that prison environment. I thought about how strange our lives turned out. I would have never believed that one day I'd be visiting my son in jail for murder charges."

Whenever my mother visited Aaron, she never knew what they would talk about—or whether Aaron would be angry, happy, sad, spiritual, or ambivalent. On some visits, she couldn't wait to leave; on other occasions she never wanted her time with Aaron to end. It all depended on Aaron's mood, which was unpredictable. What hurt her the most was saying good-bye after a positive interaction with Aaron.

This conversation began with a normal exchange of pleasantries.

"How are you doing, Aaron?" my mom asked from her side of the scratched Plexiglas.

"I'm good. You look good, Mom," Aaron said.

At first, Aaron was aglow, a big smile stretching across his face.

Aaron continued, his smile slowly disappearing even as he tried to hold it. "You don't know me, Mom."

"How could I possibly know more than you show or tell me," my mom said. "I'm not a mind reader."

"Do you remember when we used to get dropped off at the babysitter's house near the cul-de-sac?" Aaron asked.

"Yes," she said.

Aaron finally told her about one of the demons that had been haunting him all these years. He told her how the older boy would force him to perform oral sex. Aaron said it started when he was six years old and continued for several years.

"Why didn't you tell me, Aaron?" our mom said as she began to sob. "I could have protected you."

"I was afraid," Aaron said, as he put his head down and began to cry. "There's more."

For the rest of their time together, Aaron spoke in a whisper, occasionally just mouthing the words to our mother, so the officers and other visitors couldn't hear.

"Mom, I'm gay," Aaron said.

"Oh, Aaron," my mom said, still crying. "I can't even imagine having to hide this."

"My biggest fear was the thought of someone finding out," Aaron said. "Growing up, Tanya was the only person who knew. She was the only one who knew for a long time."

"Oh my gosh, Aaron."

"I've been hiding my true love from everyone," Aaron said. "Before I was even a teenager, we had sleepovers together and sometimes we would just cuddle and sleep with each other. As we got older, I'd go over to his house and we'd go into his bedroom and fool around. I saw him whenever I could. Once I was in the NFL, I'd call him every day after practice. If he was free, I'd go see him, and we'd just cuddle and talk for hours. I wanted to leave the league so we could start a life together."

Aaron said that in order to become intimate with a woman, he needed to be extremely drunk. He loved Shayanna, but it had crushed him that he couldn't give her the intimacy that she deserved. Aaron said he would stay out late with his friends, hoping that she would be asleep when he returned.

"I hated living a secret, and I hated all the lies, but I felt like I had to do all those things because people wouldn't accept me," Aaron said. "There was no way I could come out as an NFL player.

"I know it's wrong and that men aren't supposed to be gay," Aaron whispered. "You think I like being this way? I don't. If it got out in jail that I was gay, I'd be killed."

Aaron told our mother that he didn't want me to know either of his secrets. "I can't let DJ down," Aaron said.

"Aaron, your brother loves you regardless of anything," my mother said. "You should tell him."

"I can't, Mom," he said. "I don't want to let anyone in our family down. I don't want to let my friends down. And I don't want to let the fans I have left down. I just can't."

"I love you more than ever," my mom said.

Tears in his eyes, Aaron said, "I love you, too, Mom."

Then a prison guard said time was up. The visit was over.

Aaron wiped his tears, stood up, and hardened his demeanor before walking back and joining the other inmates.

CHAPTER 36

MARCH 2017

FIVE MONTHS HAD PASSED since Aaron had opened up to our mother, and now I was going to see him for the first time since he had let his walls down. I walked through the prison's thick green doors, down the narrow hallway, and sat on the stool. In the non-contact visitors' room, on the other side of Plexiglass divide, Aaron appeared.

Before Aaron picked up his phone, I wanted to blurt out: *I'm here for you. Your sexual preference does not matter to me. My love for you is unconditional.*

But I didn't. With the phone to his ear, Aaron sat down, subdued. I asked him how he was doing.

"It's Groundhog Day," he said. "Every single day is the same."

Aaron had to open up and give me the chance to listen—he had told our mom not to tell anyone, but it was too much for her to handle by herself, so she phoned me. Hearing the news had been horrifying. I was angry that I had been blind to the molestation, his hurt and his inner conflict. I hadn't protected my brother. It devastated me to learn how much pain Aaron's secrets were causing him.

In the visiting room, Aaron didn't have much to say, so I started telling stories from our childhood. He looked at me like someone who was hearing this information for the first time. He tilted his head to the left, but his eyes were focused on something past me, through me, mimicking that thousand-mile stare he had on the rooftop in Los Angeles.

I could feel his pain on the other side of the glass. He looked lost. Aaron never opened up to me.

RETURNING TO MY MOM'S condo, I felt like I needed to be closer to Aaron. There was a distance growing between us that made me uneasy.

I started to think that I should move home. But back in Dallas, Karen was three months pregnant. I wasn't going to make any major decisions until our baby was born.

CHAPTER 37

NOVEMBER 4, 2016

Two days before Aaron's twenty-seventh birthday, Karen and I checked into Texas Health Presbyterian Hospital in Dallas. We sat in the waiting room and spotted another family who had sleeping bags spread across the floor. It looked like they were tailgating or waiting in line for coveted concert tickets. I pictured what the scene would look like if my childhood family had been with us: my father would be crying, my mother would be next to him, Aaron would be at my side, and my aunts and uncles would be pacing the halls waiting for updates.

Karen was in a lot of pain. Sitting next to her, I felt helpless because I was unable to ease her discomfort. Doctors came in and out of the room, and at one point they asked me to step into the hallway so they could give Karen an epidural. I knew what an epidural was because of how often my brother was given one for his ongoing back pain in football. The birth was getting closer.

We were guided to another room because it was almost time to start pushing. I was getting nervous, all I wanted was for Karen and the baby to be healthy. I could feel Karen's pain as she squeezed my hand during contractions.

Suddenly I felt like a cheerleader. "Babe, I can see her head," I said. "She is coming; keep pushing, babe. Keep pushing."

I was so excited I didn't know what to do. I looked back up at

Karen and said, "Keep breathing, keep pushing. I can see her shoulders, babe."

I couldn't take my eyes off Parker, as the nurse raised her to Karen. I was in awe. Karen had a look on her face I had never before seen—one of accomplishment, exhaustion, and maternal love.

Parker weighed six pounds, three ounces. She was so precious. A nurse put a diaper on her. Parker looked like a little peanut with a hat.

A nurse took us to a private room on the maternity ward, and I held Parker for the first time. It was perfect. Like many new dads, I worried about dropping her, but I held on. For the first time, I knew what Aaron meant when he said that he didn't want anyone to drop his princess, because now, with Parker in my arms, I didn't want anything to happen to her. I never wanted to let go.

Two days later, we loaded Parker into her car seat, buckled her in, and then drove home. I was the slowest driver on the freeway, the cars racing past us as we turtled along in the slow lane. I constantly checked the rearview mirror. Karen's face hovered over the car seat with the biggest smile I had ever seen.

CHAPTER 38

MARCH 2017

FOUR MONTHS LATER, I was in my office at Ledyard High School in Ledyard, Connecticut, when my phone rang. I had only been on the job for four weeks—I was the head football coach and an academic and behavioral support supervisor—and during my interview I promised the superintendent that Aaron's situation wouldn't be a distraction or bring unwanted publicity to the school.

I answered the phone. "Two officers are en route to the school to speak with you about your brother," the school principal said.

Aaron's second trial began one month earlier, and I had no idea why police officers would want to visit me. I wondered if I had made the right decision to move my family back to Connecticut a month earlier to be closer to Aaron and my mother. The principal popped her head into my classroom.

"The two officers are waiting for you in an office just a few doors down," she said.

I entered the room, shut the door behind me, and shook the officers' hands. "How can I help?" I asked.

THE TRIAL FOR AARON'S double murder had started on February 14, 2017. I didn't know anything except what Aaron had told me; he couldn't believe he was even going to trial for this. The prosecution alleged that in July 2012, Aaron was at a Boston nightclub when Daniel de Abreu spilled a drink on Aaron. They claimed that two hours later, Aaron, enraged over the incident, opened fire from his silver Toyota 4Runner on De Abreu's silver BMW, killing De Abreu and Safiro Furtado.

The officers who met me at Ledyard read a packet of information that stated the date and time they wanted me to appear at Suffolk County Courthouse—March 23, 2017, at 9:30 a.m. Prosecutors wanted to speak with me.

A few days later, I went to the courthouse at 3 Pemberton Square in Boston to meet with prosecutors. I took a seat in a small room at a rectangular wooden table. Then Assistant District Attorney Patrick Haggan entered.

"I just want to ask you a few questions about your brother. I'm not sure whether or not I'll call you to the stand. I understand how much your family has been through and I know you just accepted a position at Ledyard High School."

On a TV monitor, he displayed images of Aaron's tattoos. He asked me if I knew the meaning of his various tattoos, which covered his body from neck to toe. "I have a lot going on in my life," I said. "And studying my brother's tattoos isn't one of them. He has too many for me to keep track of." I told the officer I only knew of a few.

"Do you know of any nicknames that your brother went by?" he asked.

"Yes," I said. "I call him 'Air' at times, which is short for Aaron, and his teammates called him 'Chico.' I have no idea why they called him that."

He then read off a list of nicknames. I told him I didn't recognize any of them.

"Would you mind listening to a recorded phone conversation to see if you can identify the voices?"

"Sure," I said.

He played the conversation on a computer. It was a conversation between my brother and mother, which was what I told him.

He then asked how everything was going at the school. "Good," I said. He mentioned that he grew up close to Ledyard, and we talked about the area. He said that he would let me know if I'd be called to the stand.

I had chosen not to be in the courtroom for the first few weeks of Aaron's second trial. It felt like I was being pulled in two directions. Half of me wanted to see Aaron's face, to make eye contact with him, to let him know through my presence that I loved him. But the other half of me couldn't do it. The thought of stepping in that courtroom made my body pulse harder and shake.

Over the weekend, after being interviewed by the prosecution, one of Aaron's lawyers, Ronald Sullivan, called and told me that Aaron would really like to see me in court. I told him I was planning on attending and was going to see if any other family members would want to join me.

He also asked me what I knew about his tattoos. I told him I knew the meaning of only a few. He told me that the prosecution was trying to link Aaron to the murders by his tattoos, specifically one of a gun chamber they believed Aaron had gotten that commemorated the crime. Aaron's defense team argued that the tattoo was just one of many he had put on his body because he liked the look.

"Aaron was addicted to tattoos," I told one of Aaron's lawyers. "There was a time I asked Aaron about a particular tattoo and what it meant. He said, 'I don't know, but it looks cool and I got the same tattoo a few times.'" Dating back to when Aaron was a kid, he loved to cover his body with fake tattoos. His obsession never stopped.

Aaron's lawyer thanked me and said the prosecutors wanted to call me to the stand to give the impression that I was testifying against Aaron. Then, a few days later, he sent me a text saying that I was not going to have to speak at the trial. I was beyond relieved.

CHAPTER 39

APRIL 2017

On April 1, with the trial nearing its conclusion, I called my mother and asked if she would go to support Aaron with me. "I can't do it again," she said. "One murder trial was enough. I can't do two. I can't hurt like that anymore."

I begged her, but she was adamant about not attending.

On April 3, I began my morning leading the Ledyard football team in spring workouts. Then, after showering in the coaches' locker room, I changed into my jacket and tie, and met three family members in the school's parking lot—my uncles David and Vito and my aunt Lisa. Together we drove to the courthouse in Boston.

On the way, I thought about the magnitude of this case. If Aaron was found guilty again, he would never come home. If he was innocent, he then would have a chance to appeal the Odin Lloyd case and seek a new trial.

We arrived at court and sat on Aaron's side. Once the testimony for the day ended, I waited in my seat hoping Aaron would turn around. He remained facing forward until one of his lawyers whispered into his ear to tell him we were present. Aaron stood up from his chair, looked at us, and quietly mouthed "thank you" over and over, his eyes traveling to each of us. He then looked back at me and flashed a smile—one that brought me back to Greystone. "I love you," he mouthed. We stared at each other for several long seconds.

"I love you, Air," I mouthed back.

I watched him as he walked out of the courtroom. I wanted to soak this time up. I hadn't seen him in ten months. But then, too fast, he was gone, the door closing behind him.

AFTER ATTENDING ONE DAY of trial—I was the only certified coach on staff, which meant the kids wouldn't be able work out if I wasn't present—I received a text on April 5 stating that closing arguments would begin.

The prosecution's main witness was Alexander Bradley, aka Sherrod. He testified that he pulled up to the side of a silver BMW and from the passenger's seat Aaron leaned out of the driver's-side window and began shooting into the car. Aaron's team of lawyers, led by Jose Baez, poked holes in Sherrod's testimony, questioning the authenticity of his statements and the quality of his character.

Aaron and I didn't talk on the phone during the trial, at the request of his lawyers. But the one time I met with Aaron's lawyers, they told me that the prosecution was desperate and the case against Aaron was weak. I had no idea what the jury would decide, especially following the guilty verdict from Aaron's first trial.

AFTER WORK ON APRIL 14, Karen was driving and I was in the passenger's seat on our way to an appointment to look at an apartment. I received a text from my mother telling me that the verdict was in. I went to a link on Twitter and watched it live. Staring into my iPhone screen, I heard "Not guilty; not guilty."

Aaron was nodding his head up and down as he began to cry. I was taken by my brother's emotion. I realized that we now had a slim chance to one day be reunited outside the prison walls.

ON SATURDAY, APRIL 15—ONLY one day after the verdict—Karen, Parker, and I drove to my mother's condo for Easter weekend. That afternoon we went to the Westfarms mall so we could take pictures of Parker with the Easter Bunny for the first time. Waiting in line, I couldn't believe it: a few feet away in front of us was Avielle, Shay's mother, and Shay's younger sister.

We all hugged and I just stared at Avielle. My mother smiled the entire time, saying over and over, "I know your daddy loves you. I know your daddy loves you." We took a picture—me holding Parker and Shay's younger sister holding Avielle. In that instant, I felt happiness, pain, and the distance that had grown between all of us.

The next day, Easter Sunday, my mother came running into the condo from the garage. She had her phone on speaker. It was the voice of the automated recording from jail preparing us to receive a call from Aaron.

Then Aaron said, "Hello."

"You did it, you did it!" my mother shouted. "I'm so happy for you." She told Aaron about Parker and Avielle seeing each other at the mall for the first time and started talking about how excited she was for Aaron and his lawyers to start working on his appeal in the Odin Lloyd case.

"Slow down, Mom," he said. "Let's just enjoy this outcome right now."

My mom handed me the phone. "Congratulations," I said. "I love you more than anything in the world. I'm going to come visit you soon."

"I love the both of you," Aaron said. "I don't have much time left, and I need to call Shay and Avielle." And the call ended.

THREE DAYS LATER, ON April 19, 2017, my brother died by suicide in his prison cell.

CHAPTER 40

APRIL 2017

On April 23, 2017, the funeral director at O'Brien Funeral Home in Bristol pointed down the long hallway, past the wooden chairs, and at the same white French doors that led to the room that had housed our father's casket nearly eleven years earlier.

I pulled the door open and immediately shifted my eyes to the right, away from my brother's body. I couldn't look at Aaron. I wasn't ready. I moved to the back of the room, behind the eight rows of chairs, where I paced and paced and paced, trying to build up the courage to kneel by his side.

I slowly stepped closer. I reached the casket and looked at my brother for the first time. I saw his stiff hands interlocked on his chest, his sunken cheeks, and his scrunched little forehead. I lowered to my knees.

For thirty minutes, I rested my head on his chest and closed my eyes. So many snapshots of Aaron flashed in my head: his smile, his laugh, his competitiveness, and his emotional response when he heard the verdict in his second trial. Holding him, tears rolled down my cheeks, dripping onto his chest. I whispered, "I love you Aaron. I love you Aaron. I love you Aaron."

Still kneeling, I raised my head and noticed a petite shadow appear through the long white curtains covering the window behind my brother. I had asked my mother to give me an hour alone with Aaron, and it was now her time to join us. I gave Aaron a kiss on his cold forehead as I rubbed my right hand over his thin black hair. It was time to back away from the casket.

Wearing dark cat-eye sunglasses, my mother entered the room. She turned her face to Aaron, paused, and then looked at me. My emotions erupted; I started bawling and wiping tears away with my hands.

My mom removed her shades and took several hesitant steps closer to Aaron's body. She fell to the kneeler cushion in front of the casket, dropped her neck down, and began to rub Aaron's right hand. Sitting in a chair a few feet away, I buried my head in my hands and quietly asked, "Why did you have to leave us, Aaron? Why?"

CHAPTER 41

DECEMBER 2017

On December 15, I pulled out of my driveway in Pawcatuck, Connecticut, and steered through the snow in search of answers. The day my brother passed, my mother signed forms to release Aaron's brain to the "brain bank" run by the U.S. Department of Veterans Affairs, Boston University, and the Concussion Legacy Foundation in Jamaica Plain, Massachusetts.

I needed to connect the dots, to understand my brother's erratic behavior. I sought out Dr. Ann McKee, the director of the foundation and the nation's foremost expert on chronic traumatic encephalopathy—CTE.

I drove to the hospital in Jamaica Plain. Could detailed stories of my brother's life help Dr. McKee and other doctors better understand CTE? Would this information help other families whose loved ones were experiencing similar symptoms?

I had read news reports detailing how Dr. McKee had found that Aaron suffered the most severe case of CTE ever discovered in a person his age. She had said that the brain damage was most severe in the frontal lobes of his brain, a brain area critical to decision-making, judgment, and cognition.

CTE is a degenerative brain disease most commonly found in football players, soldiers, and other individuals who have experienced repeated blows to the head. Aaron had been diagnosed with severe CTE, stage 3 out of four possible stages. Stage 3 CTE is usually found in football players who pass away at the median age of sixty-seven and played at least a decade in the NFL.

Aaron wasn't a ten-year NFL veteran. He played in only three NFL seasons—thirty-eight total games—and he was only twenty-seven years old. Aaron is one of the hundreds of former athletes who are part of the VA-BU-CLF brain bank and have been diagnosed with CTE. Were Aaron's problems in life—depression, sudden aggression, impulsivity, impaired moral judgment, memory loss, difficulty planning and carrying out tasks, substance abuse, suicidal thoughts or behavior—clinical features of CTE? Were these difficulties found in other football players diagnosed with CTE?

Aaron began playing tackle football at age seven, and he missed only one season, eighth grade because he weighed too much to participate in the league. His NFL career was short, but in total, he played tackle football for more than fifteen years. He played in more than 130 youth, high school, collegiate, and NFL games combined. His long-playing career put him at a high risk for CTE.

How many blows to the head did he take in his career? What is CTE's magic number? How many hits does it take until a brain is damaged? Does it matter that he started to play football at such a young age?

I took a seat in Dr. McKee's office at Boston Medical Center. She showed me images and slides of Aaron's brain, explaining that, if Aaron had lived, he was "most likely ten years away from being totally impaired."

Thirty minutes into our conversation, I started to tell Dr. McKee some of Aaron's personal history.

"There were times as early as second and third grade when we would be playing video games and Aaron would just snap," I said. "He would take his Sega Genesis controller and beat me with it."

"Anything before that?" she asked.

"The top of a hammer hit him in the head when he was about

eight," I said. "He dropped to the ground. Blood came out of his ears and nose."

"Did he go to the hospital?"

"No. We were both very young," I said. "I brought him inside and did my best to help clean him up."

"Was he normal at birth?" she asked. "Did he hit his milestones for crawling and walking and talking?"

"Everything was normal, according to my mother," I said.

"You noticed these episodes when he would snap?"

"He'd have episodes where he'd say, 'D, it's like I black out,'" I said. "He'd cry afterward."

"This happen frequently?"

"About four or five times."

"You didn't think this was him having a short temper?" she asked.

"It usually built up and then it was like a light switch went off inside of him."

"Was he good in school?"

"He was lazy at times but was very smart and an honor roll student."

"Do you remember any time when Aaron saw stars after he was hit?"

"No, but he was diagnosed with one concussion in high school. I remember him becoming frustrated because he couldn't return to the game."

"What else can you tell me about Aaron's childhood?"

I detailed the night terrors when Aaron woke up yelling, "They're going to get me! They're going to get me!"

"Did he walk around in his sleep?" she asked.

"Yes. He was in his own little world when he'd have these episodes. This was in second and third grade."

"So he was having nightmares and he didn't remember those night terrors."

"He didn't remember," I said.

"Did you ever notice a big change in Aaron?"

"The first time I noticed a big change in him was when I went to his house and saw that he was sleeping next to a knife. This was in March 2012."

I described seeing the bags filled with marijuana at his condo and how he was convinced that people were after him.

"This is way beyond normal paranoia," she said. "According to research, he sounds affected by CTE at that point."

I told Dr. McKee that Aaron once asked me at a bar in Boston why I was talking to a college friend. I told him we were buddies, but for the rest of the night Aaron looked at him suspiciously, keeping his eyes on him for an extended period of time.

"That's really important," she said. "According to our experience with CTE in over three hundred and fifty brains, I would say that it is very likely that he's impaired at this point. Listening to you, the symptoms of CTE probably started in high school. We have found CTE in some high school football players. According to what you are telling me, it may have started earlier than high school with the early exposure to tackle football. CTE may have been developing in his brain and affecting his thought process by age twenty-two. Although we know that CTE is related to repeated blows to the head, there may be other factors that put Aaron at a higher risk for CTE, such as specific susceptibility genes, but at this point we don't know."

"I became paranoid from his paranoia," I said. "Something seemed wrong with him and I didn't want to be around him. I assumed his paranoia was a result of the weed he had on him."

I told her about the night Aaron threw his mattress out of his bedroom because he couldn't find his cell phone and how he apologized the next morning.

"So a trivial thing and he has this very exaggerated reaction," she said. "He seems really out of control. He sounds really frightening."

"Aaron said he was actually happy in jail for a period of time," I said. "He thought being in prison brought the family back together. But he also said he would have ended it a long time ago if it wasn't for his family."

"He clearly sounds affected by CTE," she said. "People with this condition can be very obsessive and paranoid. He sounds self-aware that something is wrong but that he can't control it."

I then explained that Aaron was repeatedly molested beginning at age six by an older male that we knew.

"That can be extremely damaging psychologically," she said. "He could have suffered from post-traumatic stress disorder. PTSD can have many residual effects, including nightmares. His early problems with an explosive temper may have been caused by PTSD. The stress can cause changes in your brain's wiring and can have very profound effects. Just imagine what he's trying to deal with."

"And unfortunately there's more," I said. "Aaron grew up sexually curious. And in our household our dad said, 'There are no faggots in our family.' "

"I just can't imagine what he was going through," she said. "You just feel for him. He was going through so much."

I explained to Dr. McKee that near the end of his life Aaron's memory appeared to be getting worse. I told her that on my last prison visit I shared childhood stories with Aaron, but he didn't connect with them. He just stared at me with a blank look on his face, not remembering experiences from his own life that we discussed often.

"For such a young guy, that's a profound change in his cognition which correlates with the high severity of CTE in his brain," she said. "We've never seen anything this bad with anyone under the age of forty-five, and I've seen a lot of damaged brains."

Dr. McKee emphasized that she didn't have all the answers and that it will take years of more research to fully understand CTE. She added, "One thing we did note about Aaron was that the clearance system in his brain—it's like a garbage network that clears out the bad protein and it primarily works at night when you sleep—his clearance system was almost nonexistent. That may be part of it. I don't know why his clearance system was so bad but it was."

I asked her about the correlation between tackle football and CTE.

"The evidence is mounting," she said. "I do think football is really dangerous, especially for kids. The problem is, we can't see the brain getting damaged. The brain is floating. You have tremendous movement of the brain when you have a collision in football. The brain stretches and tears the internal structures of the brain. The blood vessels and nerve cells get torn. Also, our research has also shown that if you start playing tackle football before twelve, the damage may be worse. CTE starts very focally but over time the disease spreads to affect large regions of the brain."

"CTE wasn't even on the forefront of my mind when Aaron died," I said.

"CTE starts as small lesions in areas by the traumatic head blows, but over time, the lesions expand and can spread to other parts of the brain," she said. "Once CTE is triggered, even if you don't play football anymore, it will continue to get worse. CTE lesions are composed of an abnormal protein, called tau. At some point, the tau protein can spread to invade other brain cells. Many CTE lesions were in Aaron's frontal and temporal lobes and amygdala, and it also looked as though the tau protein was spreading to other parts of the brain. If Aaron had lived longer, I think he would have become more impaired and had difficulties accomplishing daily activities. His CTE was spreading.

"A person with CTE can become uncontrollably angry. They may have loss of memory. They may have social withdrawal and depression. Impulsivity is common. So is loss of control. And there were moments that you've described when Aaron just lost control. There is usually some degree of self-awareness, and it is likely that Aaron was aware that he couldn't control all of his behaviors and thoughts. That is very disabling for a person. He couldn't control his mind and he had to fight tremendous impulses. From what you describe it sounds like he was losing his ability to think clearly."

"What about his suicidal thoughts?" I asked. "Does CTE help explain that?"

"Aaron had all sorts of psychological and social factors that were contributing to his problems. You have this superego that tells you when something is a bad idea; the superego resides in the frontal lobes. Aaron had tremendous damage in his frontal lobes, which would have caused his judgment to be impaired.

"We have never said that this disease caused his suicide. I'll say this: with the amount of frontal lobe damage he had, research has shown that it would have been very difficult for Aaron to make decisions. He had nobody internally, so to speak, saying that he shouldn't do this and he shouldn't do that. This raises a question of his competence.

"In terms of his suicide—how competent was he to make a good decision? I would say he was impaired."

CHAPTER 42

MARCH 2018

On March 22, 2018—nearly a year after Aaron's passing—I sat in my SUV outside the Massachusetts State Police office in Worcester. I was hesitant to go inside to meet with Detective Lieutenant Allan D. Hunt and Trooper James J. Foley. I feared the pain, the nightmares, and the overpowering thoughts resurfacing, but I knew it was what I needed to do to find closure.

Inside, I asked if I could view some of the images from Aaron's cell. Trooper Foley opened his laptop, rotated the screen toward me, and then slid the laptop to my side of the table. Suddenly, I was staring at my brother's world, cell #57.

There was a window in the farthest right corner on the back wall. I saw a long white bedsheet intertwined and knotted around the bars on the window. My eyes traveled down the sheet to the dirty, brownish smear on the cement floor. The bottle of shampoo my brother poured out on the floor had become discolored from the circular rings of blood he had drawn on the bottom of his feet. I imagined him fighting the pain as his feet slipped out from underneath him.

Below the window was a cement slab he used as a chair at his desk. His stool had something on it. I rotated the computer around and asked Trooper Foley to zoom in. It looked like two pennies. I wondered if they were resting heads up—and if the positioning of them had any significance.

The top of his desk was clear. Beneath it, on the ground, books were piled in stacks. I wished I could have visited my brother moments before he ended his life and say, "Aaron, please don't leave us."

I thought about how different this life had turned out from the one we had envisioned on the hill as children. I felt the hurt build inside me, like I was losing him again in those pictures and I couldn't do anything about it.

I focused on the big silver trunk labeled "G2 57" up against the white wall on the right side of the room—the same trunk Aaron brewed his strong coffee on, and where he stored his personal belongings, including letters I wrote to him.

In the farthest left corner of his room, about four feet above the cement floor, I saw the two white drawstring netted bags with Aaron's white clothes in them. The third hook from the left was empty, but on the forth hook was a long-sleeve black shirt. It hung there, lifeless.

My eyes moved to his bed. I imagined him placing his four cups of water on the floor to drink during the night before making pillows by folding his shirts neatly at the far end of his bed. I thought about the nightmares he said he still had.

I saw a plastic jar of peanut butter, packages of "Oodles of Noodles," and snacks under his bed, the side closest to his cell door. I saw an empty plastic bottle with its label peeled off lying sideways in the middle of the room.

A plastic spoon was on the floor. I wondered if he used the corner of the spoon to slit his right middle finger so he could mark his forehead and Bible with blood.

The word "ILLUMINATI" was written to the right of the silver trunk positioned on the floor.

I saw all I needed to see; I slid the computer back to the other side of the table. Aaron was not visible in any of the photos.

I asked if I could read the suicide letters that had been left on the floor, to the right of his open Bible. An officer grabbed a manila folder, pulling out one of Aaron's last letters.

As my eyes traveled over the final word "GODBODY" and the two halos, the officers leaned over to me and asked if I knew what it meant—I didn't. Everything was happening so fast. I didn't know what to think. I was still struggling to erase the mental image of my brother dangling from his bedsheet.

I was more lost, more hurt, than when I entered the interrogation room. The officers were very informative and helpful, but I now had more questions. Why didn't my brother say good-bye? Was he mad at me? I became pissed at myself, because I didn't do more for him when I had the chance.

My body shook. I felt more information was out there. Something inside me was telling me to keep going, to keep searching. I wondered if someone was hiding information my brother left behind.

I drove to the office of the district attorney, five minutes away. Walking up the hill to the front door, I didn't hear the traffic or the sounds of construction or the flag snapping back and forth on the flagpole.

I was directed through the security entrance. I went past the big white pillars and stairs leading to courtrooms above on the balcony. I stood silent inside the elevator going down to the office.

I entered the doors to the DA's office and walked up to the counter. A woman rose from her chair and asked how she could help. I told her that I had just finished meeting with two officers and they advised me to come here to gain access to the information I was seeking.

"My name is Jonathan Hernandez. I'm Aaron Hernandez's biological brother. I'd like to meet with the district attorney."

"I'm afraid he's in a meeting," she said.

I told her I didn't mind waiting. I was desperate for more information.

The lady stepped away to make a call, then returned to the front counter, handed me her business card, and told me the district attorney should be back in about an hour. After thanking her, I walked back upstairs. I felt like I had been given surface information since the day my brother passed. I needed to see and hear everything with my own eyes and ears.

Forty-five minutes later, I walked through security again, past the pillars again, and into the DA's office. An older gentleman with glasses wearing a dark-blue suit noticed me and approached. The assistant DA said hello and offered me his hand.

I followed him past the front desk and a warren of cubicles into his office.

"I'm sorry for your loss," he said. "How can I help you?"

"I just met with two officers and they said you may be able to help me find the answers I'm looking for," I said. "I would like to see any documents you have regarding my brother because I know it would help me find closure."

He escorted me across the hall to a conference room, where empty chairs surrounded a rectangular table. The walls had old paintings of former district attorneys. He left and then, a few moments later, the door opened behind me. He placed Aaron's prison history documents on the table. He told me to take all the time I needed.

At first, I stared at the packets trying to memorize every word. I realized I was studying information I had at home—packets I had filed in my office, information detailing his death and his time in prison.

Then I saw the letters—Aaron's final letters.

I began to read. My body squeezed tight. I felt Aaron's anguish and hurt through his words as he briefly described the severity of the pain in his life. As I was reading, it was as if I could feel loneliness, his life passing him by, him letting go.

AFTERWORD

In June 2018, I sat in Coach Randy Edsall's office—in the same leather chair at UConn, where eleven years earlier I had opened up to my former coach about my own struggles.

During our conversation, I was silently gripped by the thought of my brother. What if Aaron had shared his problems with someone who could have helped him before it was too late? Would his story have been different?

Before my brother was incarcerated, he appeared to have it all—a fiancé, a healthy daughter, a $40 million contract, and a smile that could light up a stadium. But the brightness of his smile blinded me. Only now do I understand that on the inside, he was full of self-loathing—an anger that built up over the years because he never reached out for the help he needed. He didn't enjoy his life because every time he looked in the mirror he couldn't accept the reflection.

Every day I ask myself if I could have done more for Aaron—or was his brain already too impaired from CTE? Or was it something else perhaps that no one knew?

I think back to our time in our childhood living room—what if our family had turned off the television? Would we have discussed our feelings and emotions? Would my brother have been more comfortable sharing his pain rather than living in fear of what his family members, friends, teammates, and fans thought of him? Would my young brother still be alive today?

It is my sincere hope that this book—Aaron's truth—will be a source of motivation, one that propels others to appreciate life's blessings, to seek help during difficult times, and to work on finding inner-happiness.

ACKNOWLEDGMENTS

WORDS CANNOT FULLY EXPRESS how appreciative I am for Lars Anderson's friendship. Writing this book with him has been an emotional process, and without his patience and support, I don't know if we would have been able to successfully complete a project that is so close to my heart. His ability to delicately challenge me to share the moments in my life I had worked so hard to bury has helped me move forward.

Scott Waxman, my agent, believed in this story from the very beginning. He patiently read several drafts of the book proposal and each time gave me valuable feedback. This book wouldn't have happened without his leadership, dedication, and guidance.

Luke Dempsey, my executive editor at Harper, shared my vision for the book. His energy and attention to detail are inspiring. Thank you, Luke. And this project wouldn't have been possible without the dedication of the entire team at Harper, including assistant editor Haley Swanson, deputy general counsel Beth Silfin, publicist Leslie Cohen, production editor Nate Knaebel, interior designer Fritz Metsch, and cover designer James Iacobelli.

Sheila and Gerry Levine, my lawyers, helped me navigate the world of literary contracts. Thank you both.

My father, Dennis Hernandez, taught me the value of family. Dad, you will always be with me.

My coaches and teammates at UConn helped me through some difficult times. The relationships I formed during college remain special because of the growth we experienced together. I love you all.

Iowa coach Kirk Ferentz allowed me to become a member of the Hawkeye family. If it weren't for the people inside that building in Iowa City, I would not be here today. In my darkest days, the program became the family I desperately needed in my life. At the time, I didn't realize how vital they were to my emotional recovery, but now—after writing this book and reliving the difficult events of my past—I want everyone a part of the Hawkeye program to know how much you still mean to me. I'm especially in debt to Coach Greg Davis, Coach Brian Ferentz, Coach Bobby Kennedy, Coach Chris White, Coach Joel Welsh, and Coach Chris Polizzi. I also want to thank author and Iowa professor Travis Vogan for his support and inspiration to continue writing.

Mike Bakaysa, my former high school coach, and his entire family treated me like a son. I'll never forget the times you invited me into your house to spend time with your family. Thank you all for being a constant in my life.

Jim Buonocore, the assistant principal and athletic director at Ledyard High School, gave me a chance when my brother was in the national news virtually every day. Thank you for believing in me.

Chad Lockhart, thank you for helping me bring my visions, emotions, and ideas to life through your art.

My family, including my mother, Terri, provided me with the support that allowed me to write this book. Thanks for always being a phone call away.

To my wife, Karen, and daughter, Parker, you two are the best teammates I've ever had in my life. I will forever appreciate the sacrifices you both made to allow me the time to complete this book. Thank you for understanding how much this project means to me. I love you both with all my heart.

Finally, to Aaron, my best friend. I love you—always.

ABOUT THE AUTHORS

JONATHAN HERNANDEZ WAS a starting quarterback at Bristol Central High School, where he was named Connecticut's Gatorade Player of the Year in 2003. He went on to play at the University of Connecticut, where he became a two-time team captain and earned his master's degree in educational psychology. He later had coaching stints at Southington High School (2009–10), Brown University (2011), the University of Miami (2012), and the University of Iowa (2013–14), and was the head coach at Ledyard High School (2017).

LARS ANDERSON IS A *New York Times* bestselling author of eight books. A twenty-year veteran of *Sports Illustrated*, he is a contributing writer to the *Athletic*.